Critical Skills
in the Early Years

Vicki Charlesworth

NetworkEducationalPress

Published by
Network Educational Press Ltd
PO Box 635
Stafford
ST16 1BF

First published 2005

ISBN-13:   978 1 85539 184 0
ISBN-10:   1 85539 184 8

Editor: Debbie Pullinger
Design: Andy Wilson

Printed in Great Britain by Ashford Colour Press Ltd, Gosport, Hants.

Contents

Chapter 5 A sequence of challenges and the introduction of roles

Chapter 6 Feedback and assessment

Chapter 7 Linking Critical Skills to early years practice

Chapter 8 Progressive indicators of achievement

Teachers' resources to accompany this book are available on the CD-ROM which can be found on the inside back cover. An icon in the margin indicates there is a resource related to that section. A list of these resources can be found on page 129.

Foreword

The Critical Skills Programme meets many of the needs of teaching in the twenty-first century: engaging the learner, offering a challenge to teachers and pupils alike, encouraging teamwork and effective communication, invoking imagination and creativity. Our evaluation of the programme in Jersey, where it has been adopted in every school, shows that there is high esteem for it from both pupils and teachers, and that there is also value in collaboration between schools. I hope this book, whose author has been involved in that island-wide collaboration, will have a significant impact on schools generally.

Ted Wragg
Professor of Education, Exeter University

Acknowledgements

The development of the Critical Skills Programme on Jersey would not have been possible without the overwhelming support of the Jersey Department for Education, Sport and Culture. In particular, the author and publisher would like to acknowledge the vision, enthusiasm and energy of Curriculum Manager Clare Downey. As Ted Wragg said in his report on the work, 'Our overall conclusion is that the Critical Skills Programme in Jersey empowers rather than inhibits teachers, enhances pupils' learning, and is appropriate for its purpose of preparing children for adult life in the twenty-first century … The vision and drive of Clare Downey have been an important part of this success.'

Chapter 1
Introduction

As a nursery class teacher, I am constantly looking for ways to enhance the learning that takes place in the classroom. How can I ensure that children are equipped with skills that will help them succeed as members of a class, school and the wider community? In particular, I have been concerned with the following questions:

☆ How can skills such as ownership, self-direction and decision making be taught to young children?

☆ How can I help children to develop mutual respect and understanding?

☆ How can I facilitate collaboration among children – rather than just co-operation?

Through the Critical Skills Programme (CSP) I have found an effective way of addressing all these questions. The programme is easy to implement with young children and is aimed at developing certain skills which they will continue to build on throughout their school lives. These 'Critical Skills' are essentially life skills, and there are eight of them:

☆ problem solving	☆ communication
☆ decision making	☆ organization
☆ critical thinking	☆ management
☆ creative thinking	☆ leadership

In addition, the programme seeks to develop seven fundamental dispositions:

☆ ownership	☆ collaboration
☆ self-direction	☆ curiosity and wonder
☆ quality	☆ community
☆ character	

Critical skills poster

Fundamental dispositions poster

No early years practitioner would deny the importance of any of these skills and dispositions: they are the life skills that are desirable in all members of society. The question is, how do we get it right? How do we ensure that the children we teach will not only have had experience of using these skills, but will have them internalized to such a degree that they will continue to develop them as they grow physically, emotionally and socially? If this issue concerns you, then the Critical Skills Programme may be the answer you've been looking for.

This book outlines a practical approach to teaching and learning in early years settings, through which the children you teach can develop into confident and independent learners who work collaboratively within a supportive learning community to solve meaningful problems or challenges.

What is the Critical Skills Programme?

The Critical Skills Programme is essentially a problem-based approach to learning. It engages children and young people in their own learning, enhances the day-to-day running of the classroom and facilitates the production of high-quality work.

The programme originated in New Hampshire in 1981, when educationalists and businesses came together in response to the report *A Nation at Risk*. They explored the following questions:

☆ What skills are vitally important for students to have by the time they leave school in order to be successful in their lives?

☆ What would a classroom be like that gave conscious and purposeful attention to the development of these skills?

☆ What skills are lacking in the workforce that impede individual and organizational success?

Through the late 1980s and early 1990s, the programme developed and spread beyond New Hampshire to Maine, New York, Vermont and Massachusetts, and continued to grow nationally throughout the 1990s. The programme – known in the United States as 'Education by Design' – was introduced to the UK in 1999 as the 'Critical Skills Programme', and in a relatively short time became established as a highly effective classroom methodology.

While the principles of CSP are described briefly below, it is not within the scope of this book to provide a full exposition of the model: for more details about the programme and how it has developed in the UK, please visit the Critical Skills website. Alternatively, the *Level 1 Coaching Kit* will give you a full account of the programme, how it is structured and what it looks like in practice.

Training on CSP is available (see Critical Skills website), and the initial course takes six days. However, while a training course will undoubtedly be helpful, it is certainly not a prerequisite for implementing some of the Critical Skills principles in an early years classroom, as described in this book.

Skills for life

Critical skills are essentially life skills. As adults functioning in society, we need to be able to make decisions, communicate, solve problems and work together harmoniously. Through CSP, children are able to experience these skills at first hand. They develop an understanding of agreed values, codes of behaviour, and expectations and aspirations for their lives. They are then able to develop their own community; they come to see the advantages of acquiring these skills and developing them through meaningful and contextual experiences.

In an ever-changing global market, workforces are constantly having to evolve and adapt. 'A job for life' is no longer a reality for most people. Employers have to adapt to meet consumer needs and to keep up to date with technological advances. To do this, they need flexible workforces and employees who can think laterally, creatively and critically. They need workforces equipped with the skills to solve problems as they arise and to make decisions where necessary. They also need workforces who think positively about challenge and change, who strive to raise standards and who reflect in order to improve. By implementing CSP in our schools, we are providing this adaptable workforce for the future.

Key principles and practice

We believe that education must be experiential, must nurture independence, and must enable all members of each generation to develop the judgement necessary to take responsibility for:

- the conduct of their lives;
- the shaping of their societies;
- and their participation in global issues.

We believe that judgement is the integration of knowledge, skills, and standards of ethical behaviour that guides decisions, commitment, and action.

Mobilia, W. (1999)

The Critical Skills classroom model is based on four educational ideas:

☆ **Experiential learning** – this means that children are given real-life problems to solve, ones that have an impact not only on their life within the classroom, but also on their life outside it.

☆ **A collaborative learning community** – in terms of the day-to-day running of the class, this is, perhaps, the most powerful aspect of the programme. CSP provides tools that allow teachers and children to develop a shared responsibility for the classroom environment and a supportive culture whereby they achieve goals together.

☆ **Standards or results-driven learning** – children in a Critical Skills classroom take part in activities designed to necessitate the demonstration of their developing knowledge and understanding and of skills and dispositions.

☆ **Problem-based learning** – the primary approach to learning is through carefully planned challenges for children to carry out. These are set within a real-life context (contextual for them), and provide them with the big picture in relation to their learning. They can see what they are doing and why they are doing it, and can see the advantages in working through a problem. Through these challenges, children have the opportunity to develop and apply their knowledge and understanding, as well as to demonstrate their critical skills and fundamental dispositions.

The Critical Skills model

The key elements in the Critical Skills model are:

The experiential cycle

Children engage in a challenge, carry it out and perform in accordance with criteria, then reflect upon what they have done and learned. This learning then connects directly to their next challenge. Thus the cycle of learning continues and children come to see exactly how learning takes place.

Taking responsibility

The Critical Skills model allows children to take control over their environment, their learning and ultimately their lives. The experiential cycle encourages them to make their own decisions and understand the consequences of their actions. It is vital that teachers coach, stand back, and intervene only when necessary. This allows children to make the decisions for themselves, taking control and experiencing responsibility at first hand. It is only by doing this that they will develop an understanding of responsibility and what it means for them.

Tools for thinking

In CSP, the development of critical skills is facilitated by a number of tools, such as brainstorming and the distillation of ideas – as illustrated here. There is more on the use of tools in Chapter 2.

Challenges

The design and use of challenges is a key element of CSP. Challenges are essentially problems that the children have to work together to solve. By taking part in challenges, the children are able to:

☆ develop understanding through performance

☆ demonstrate their developing skills and attitudes

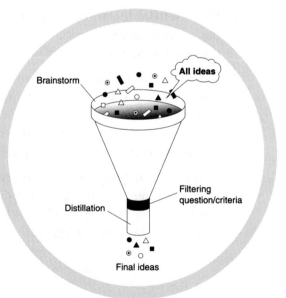

☆ attend to the processes of learning and social interaction

☆ see the big picture that makes the work worth doing.

Why implement Critical Skills in a foundation stage setting?

It may be argued that all early years practitioners see the development of social skills as paramount to the work that they do with young children, and that all good foundation stage settings are developing these skills without the aid of CSP. We all know these skills are vital, but it is not sufficient, in my opinion, to rely on their being acquired through daily social interactions and chance incidents. This book offers an approach which not only treats these skills as specific and teachable concepts, but also provides practitioners with the strategies of implementation in order to maximize learning. These strategies, activities, opportunities for observation and assessment leave nothing to chance.

A recent study into early years practice has highlighted the need for a model such as Critical Skills in the early years classroom. The EPPE research (Effective Provision of Pre-School Education) aimed, among other things, to identify characteristics of effective pre-school settings. The effectiveness of each setting was determined by the outcomes of the sample children studied. The findings showed that in the most effective settings:

☆ staff guided the learning but did not dominate it

☆ peer interactions were usually positive (e.g. co-operating and sharing)

☆ staff provided some opportunity for children to work together to complete a task.

These three descriptions exactly fit the Critical Skills model. Using this approach, children benefit from a level of 'sustained shared thinking' whereby two or more individuals work together to solve a problem. They work towards and meet early learning goals in a contextual way. Adults are involved in the process at a level that is necessary to enhance learning. This classroom dynamic nurtures independence and creates a shared responsibility among the children. The children are able to contextualize their own learning, see the big picture and understand the advantages of solving problems together. By doing this, they develop a sense of trust in one another and are able to acknowledge and celebrate success, not only in themselves, but in their peers.

What does an early years Critical Skills classroom look like?

There are nine notable characteristics of a Critical Skills classroom. This is what you would see if you walked into an early years setting that was using a Critical Skills approach.

☆ **Children frequently work as a team** – whether they are working together to construct a train track or to tidy the blocks, children are gaining the skills necessary to work as a team. This goes beyond simply working alongside others – which frequently happens in early years settings. Rather, the children actually collaborate to get a job done. This collaboration is acknowledged, highlighted and praised as a desirable behaviour which facilitates the day-to-day running of the class.

☆ **Children actively solve meaningful problems** – it is the role of the teacher to create meaningful 'problems' for the children to solve. By stopping the group and stating, 'We have a problem in the class; I need your help' the teacher is able to engage the children immediately. They are then invited to suggest solutions to whatever problem is affecting their learning. For example, the problem could be that paintings hung up to dry are falling down because there is a draught. Children are invited to think of possible solutions, which are talked through – even the seemingly unworkable ones – before a decision is reached.

☆ **Children publicly exhibit their learning** – they are given the opportunity to share their work with others. By developing a 'clapping culture', children begin to value the appreciation of their peers and are able to share with them what they have achieved. When the group is stopped to celebrate a particular success, the children are given instant feedback on their achievement, and this appreciation is modelled for the other children. A day in an early years classroom can be so hectic that it can be easy to miss achievements. It might be that a child has sampled a new food at snack time or has managed to put their coat on independently; these incidents are not overlooked. The children learn to praise one another and value their achievements.

☆ **Children reflect on what they are learning and doing** – they are given the opportunity to respond to questions such as: 'What did you do?' and 'How did you solve the problem?' This doesn't always come at the end of a challenge. In fact, it is probably more meaningful to encourage reflection all the way through the learning process, because this provides instant recognition and fosters the habit of constant reflection on the part of the children.

☆ **Children apply quality criteria to their work** – the children know what they have to achieve – and for very young children this does have to be made completely explicit. For example, if they are working together to make a boat, they need to know that it must be big enough and strong enough to carry a particular toy. These criteria are made clear from the start and referred to at various stages of the challenge. This means that the children are always aware of what they are working towards. Similarly, the quality criteria are applied to the general expectations of behaviour on a daily basis. Allowing the children to decide what constitutes 'good listening', for example, means they are more likely to achieve it because they have set an achievable standard themselves.

☆ **Teachers mediate, coach and support the learning process** – as early years practitioners, they are continually observing the children, following their leads and engaging in their play, where necessary or appropriate. These practices are easily transferred to the Critical Skills approach. Teachers observe the children, recognize the need to interact, and highlight the learning process to them. Comments such as 'I like the way you asked Sarah what she thought', or 'You made a decision: well done!' affirm the priority placed on the skills that the children are demonstrating.

☆ **Targeted learning results or standards guide the culture, the curriculum and assessment** – many if not all of the early learning goals are achievable through the Critical Skills approach, and these goals are made explicit to the children. They are told that by deciding together how their product will be made, they are learning to work as part of a group (Personal, social and emotional development). They are told that listening to someone in the group is helping them to take turns when they are talking (Communication, language and literacy). In this way, children begin to see what they are working towards. This relates to the idea of giving children the big picture to contextualize their learning for them.

☆ **Work is interconnected** – children can see that they are learning from their experiences. Referring back to prior experiences and building on these is a powerful method for enhancing learning in young children. They begin to reflect on what they did last time, how it affected them and what they will do next time as a result. This can be as simple as understanding that the day before there was not time for a story because it took longer to tidy the block area. The children may then decide either to work more quickly or to enlist more help in order to finish earlier and have time for a story. This progresses as the children complete challenges and engage in debriefing to think about what went well and what they will need to do in order to improve next time. This is the basic principle of formative assessment: establishing where you are in terms of learning, where you need to be in order to take the learning forward and coming to an understanding of how to close the gap.

☆ **Children take responsibility for and ownership of their learning and the classroom community** – they are involved in decisions which affect their learning environment. For example, if a role-play area is to be created, children are asked to list what they will need, then are helped to collect resources and to create the new area. This kind of activity results in the children taking ownership over the classroom. Similarly, if there is a problem, they are given the opportunity to solve it together. This gives them strategies for solving conflict independently, without the need for adult intervention, which is vital in a challenge situation.

Our story

I began implementing the Critical Skills model with a class of Year 4 children at Mont Nicolle Primary School in Jersey, Channel Islands. I then transferred to a group of Year 6 children, where I saw the power of this method of teaching and learning. The children took responsibility for their own learning and were able to decide what the benchmarks of quality should be for their work and their behaviour. This facilitated the smooth running of the classroom because the expectations were set by the children themselves. They agreed what would be fair, reasonable and achievable, and they were able to work towards this because it was so explicit. They understood what 'quality' meant in terms of their conversation and their ability to listen to others and be an audience, and in terms of their work. They were able to articulate the benefits of this method to their parents and visitors to the school, encouraging them to understand how they were learning and how this method made them feel. They were truly empowered by Critical Skills, and I believe that the knowledge and understanding along with the skills and dispositions that they acquired will continue to develop with them through secondary school and on into adult life, because they are, essentially, life skills.

My next challenge was to transfer the Critical Skills Programme to children at the foundation stage. The big questions were, could three and four year olds:

☆ work together to solve a problem?

☆ understand what it means to be a good listener?

☆ make decisions with their peers?

☆ take responsibility for their learning environment?

☆ appreciate their own achievements and those of others?

☆ reflect on their learning to enhance the process in the future?

The answer to all of these questions proved to be 'yes'. It is possible to implement Critical Skills in a foundation stage setting: our children are, and this book is, testament to that.

Critical Skills has enabled me to develop a culture of shared responsibility. The children know that the nursery is 'ours', and they acknowledge that they have a say in how it operates. They help out with displays because it is in their interest; they want their nursery to look attractive. They work together to tidy up because it is everyone's responsibility. They help each other because they understand what it feels like when someone helps them. They tell me when someone has let them join in a game because they appreciate how this makes them feel, and how difficult it can be to let others play. They can be heard saying things like 'I think there's a problem', and offering solutions. Our constant modelling has resulted in comments such as 'We could take turns, couldn't we?' and 'Shall we share it?' – which are amazing to hear from children who are only three and four years of age. The atmosphere in the room is calm (most of the time!) as the children are able not only to co-operate but to collaborate within the setting. They have developed what I call a clapping culture, whereby they frequently celebrate their own successes and those of their peers. I can honestly say that it is a joy to be in our Critical Skills nursery classroom.

How to use this book

It is intended that the book is followed in order, because the chapters reflect the sequence of implementation.

One of the four fundamental concepts in Critical Skills is the idea of a collaborative learning community (see page 9, above), and this is the place to start. Before the children can carry out problem-based challenges in an experiential cycle, they need to feel secure and valued as group members in a supportive culture within the classroom. Through modelling, through group and whole-class activities, and through constant reinforcing, you can begin to develop this culture in your class. For this reason, it is recommended that you begin with Chapter 2, which looks at developing the collaborative learning community. The chapter examines ways in which you can model conflict-resolution strategies, establish routines and use 'tools' to enhance learning. It provides tried-and-tested activities for whole-class and small-group community-building activities, and looks at ways to encourage a shared responsibility for the learning environment.

Chapter 3 provides an outline of a whole-class challenge which can be used to introduce the class to the format, expectations and standard operating procedures of a challenge. This is followed in Chapter 4 by details of a challenge for small groups of children. This challenge is intended for use once the children have had some experience of a challenge situation, possibly through the modelling involved in a whole-class situation.

In Chapter 5, we begin to look at assessment for learning and how we can take the learning on once a challenge is complete. Through the example of a sequence of challenges, this chapter tackles the learning cycle and introduces the concept of task roles.

Chapter 6 focuses on methods of feeding back to the children during and after a challenge, and looks at methods of formative assessment which are appropriate in the foundation stage. It details the use of puppets for assessment purposes and introduces the concept of rubrics for assessment.

Finally, Chapter 7 links the Critical Skills and fundamental dispositions (as listed on page 7) to the early learning goals of the Curriculum Guidance for the Foundation Stage document. It gives practical ways in which you can develop each skill in an everyday context, and provides child-speak scripts to facilitate this. It also includes examples of focused observations to show how these skills can be identified, acknowledged and developed in a foundation stage setting.

Chapter 2
How to develop a learning community

The development of a supportive, collaborative learning community is the backbone of all Critical Skills work. A successful classroom community works together, takes risks, supports its members, celebrates success and reflects on its learning. Get this part right, and the children will embrace any challenge you give them. If a learning community has not been established, your children will not be sufficiently equipped with the skills to facilitate the completion of a challenge.

As noted in Chapter 1, these ideas and activities are not new or original. Foundation stage teachers place great emphasis on building community as they endeavour to provide a safe and secure learning environment, where children feel settled and so on. The ideas in this book simply build on this understanding and appreciation of a classroom community.

The first steps in creating a learning community are to highlight everyday problems and to attend to problem-solving processes. Alongside these goes the development of an appreciation of process in general – in other words, valuing the decisions and actions necessary in order to produce a product. The Critical Skills focus on appreciating process – for the parents as well as the children – will facilitate the group-work which follows.

As the learning community strengthens, modelling the use of 'tools' can be introduced. These tools are strategies and processes that the children can draw on as they begin to work collaboratively.

Finally, as the children grow in confidence, you can begin experimenting with a variety of check-in activities for both small and large groups. Only do these when you feel confident and when you think the community is ready; some of them require a great deal of trust, and this does not build up overnight.

Highlight everyday problems – providing opportunities

Developing and nurturing a learning community has to be planned in an ongoing way. As well as the organized activities that help the children to work together, there are many daily incidental experiences which can be used to help create this type of environment. The emphasis on collaboration is central, and it is the role of the teacher to provide opportunities for this and to explicate the learning as it takes place. As a simple example, by having a round table for the children to sit at to have their snack, collaboration is encouraged and highlighted as someone passes the milk, or asks for an apple to be handed to them.

Identify a problem

Everyday problem solving can be introduced very early on – as soon as the children are settled into the class. Begin by looking for opportunities to highlight 'problems'. You don't need to create problems: simply use the situations that arise in the course of classroom life – for example, you might find there are several books on the floor in the quiet area. Having identified the problem, in a suitable moment bring all the children together and explain the situation. This approach has several advantages. Firstly, it helps the children to acknowledge that there is in fact a problem. Secondly, it helps them to see that it is a problem belonging to everyone in the class at that moment: it is a shared problem. Thirdly, it allows children the opportunity to suggest possible solutions. This demonstrates to them that their suggestions are valued. Fourthly, it models problem-solving strategy for those children who are happy to watch rather than be directly involved. Finally, and perhaps most importantly at this stage, it introduces the children to the language associated with problem-based learning:

- 😊 'We have a problem.'
- 😊 'What is the problem?'
- 😊 'Why is it a problem?'
- 😊 'What could we do?'
- 😊 'We have solved the problem.'

These phrases give the children the vocabulary necessary to approach and solve problems by themselves. This is, of course, vital if they are to carry out challenges in groups. Opportunities to call the children together to model the problem-solving approach could include situations such as the following:

- ☆ There are too many blocks on the carpet, and it is hard to stand up.
- ☆ It's raining but we want to go outside.
- ☆ There are only two horses in the stable, and three children would like to play in it.
- ☆ Some of the sand from the sand tray has spilled out onto the floor.
- ☆ The home corner is too untidy for children to play there.
- ☆ The hanging shells and ribbons in the trees outside keep blowing away.
- ☆ The leaves from the trees outside are filling up our drain, stopping the water from draining out of our playground.
- ☆ There are too many people in the block-play / role-play area.
- ☆ Some of the water from the water tray has spilled onto the floor.
- ☆ Stacey cannot reach the milk jug from where she is sitting at the table.

'We have a problem. There are too many blocks out and it's hard to stand up.'

In each case, state the problem and ask the children why they think it *is* a problem. This is vital if they are to offer solutions: they need to know why you are drawing their attention to the issue before they can consider how the problem might be solved.

Invite solutions

Once the existence and nature of the problem has been agreed, ask the children for their assistance: 'This is a problem. What could we do?' Encourage them to make suggestions, praising their offers of help. This can be quite tricky at first, but as the children become familiar with the process, they will become more willing and able to offer suggestions. Many of the problems highlighted may be fairly similar, and you may find the children offering the same or similar solutions to all of them. It is important to value all contributions, and to talk through even seemingly unworkable offers. In some cases, you may have several viable suggestions. This is an opportunity to show the children that there is often more than one possible solution, and that a decision may need to be made. Equally important is the concept that there is not a solution to every problem.

Problem	Possible solutions
There are too many blocks on the carpet, and it is hard to stand up.	We could put some of the blocks away so there is more room again.
	We could have fewer children in the block area.
	We could keep the crates on the shelves so there will be more carpet space.
It's raining, but we want to go outside.	We could put on our coats and boots and go out with umbrellas.
	We could stay under the canopy.
	We could go out, but only for a short time so we don't get too wet.
	We could wait until it stops raining.
There are only two horses in the stable, and three children would like to play in it.	We could take turns with the horses.
	We could buy some more horses.
	We could share them.
	We could have only two at a time playing.
Some of the sand from the sand tray has spilled out onto the floor.	We could get the dustpan and brush to sweep up the sand.
	We could try to keep it in the tray next time.
The home corner is too untidy for children to play there.	We could hang the clothes up in the home corner.
	We could tuck the chairs in.
	We could lay the table and put the babies away.
The hanging shells and ribbons in the trees outside keep blowing away.	We could ask the caretaker for some more string.
	We could move them near the fence where it isn't so windy.
	We could hang them up inside.
The leaves from the trees outside are filling up the drain, stopping the water from draining out of our playground.	We could pick up the leaves outside. We could use a brush and a wheelbarrow.
	We could ask the caretaker to clean the drain out – and we could help him.
There are too many people in the block-play / role-play area.	Some people will have to go back to their choosing board.
Some of the water from the water tray has spilled onto the floor.	We could get the mop for the water, so people don't slip.
	We could try to keep our hands over the water tray so there aren't so many drips.
Stacey cannot reach the jug of milk from where she is sitting at the snack table.	I could pass the jug across the table so that Stacey could reach it.
	She could ask a friend to pass her the jug.

Facilitate decision making

Once a solution has been offered, the children need to agree that this is the right course of action to solve the problem. Restate the suggestion so that all the children can hear it. Then ask them, for example:

- 'What do you think?'
- 'Would that work?'
- 'Could we do that?'
- 'Would that solve the problem?'

It is important to model the process of decision making in this way. The children could show agreement by putting their hands up, by standing by a particular adult or by using the thumb tool (see page 26 for more about this). Counting the number of children who agree or disagree can also work. The objective is to make it clear that everyone has had their say and that a consensus has been reached. The decision-making process is concluded by the affirmation: 'You made a decision together.' Always thank the children for their contributions. They may like to clap to celebrate their success.

Working through a conflict: 'There are five children but only one ambulance. What could we do?'

Model the importance of process

Valuing the process is one of the most important aspects of this problem-solving approach. The processes of decision making, creative thinking, organization and ownership are more important than the end product. This can be a difficult focus to shift, but it is vital if the children are to work collaboratively on challenges. There are several ways to do it.

One strategy is to display, alongside the finished products, photographs of the children working. These can be used to talk about the process and to remind the children of the stages they went through in order to complete the model, painting, sculpture or other product. An additional benefit is that parents can see for themselves the stages of involvement (as well as the usual display of outcome), and this raises their awareness of process, too.

Another strategy is to seize the opportunity when a child brings in a painting or other creation from home to show the group. When the child tells the others about their work, supply prompts such as:

- 'What did you need?'
- 'What did you need to do?'
- 'What did you decide to use?'
- 'How did you do it?'
- 'What worked well?'

In this way, the children will gradually become accustomed to describing the process as well as, or instead of, the product.

Cooking together provides a great opportunity for the children to do something for others, enhancing the sense of community within the group. It is also an opportunity to promote the importance of process. The children need to collaborate, and you can emphasize this throughout.

Establish routines through contextual problems

If children are to take risks and learn, then they need to feel secure in their environment. Part of this feeling of security comes from their taking ownership over their setting. By letting them establish their routines, you are giving children the opportunity to decide for themselves what is important and necessary in their setting.

If children are to be asked to carry out a routine, they need to see the importance of it and recognize the need for it. They should be made aware that carrying out a task in the same way every time essentially makes life easier. It is possible to make children aware of routines, to allow them the opportunity to decide upon the best systems and to reinforce the structure at a subconscious level. They are then better able to follow the routines because they have devised them themselves. And if there is a record of the routines permanently displayed for them to see, it is easy to refer back to it as necessary. In this way, a culture of collaboration is established and the children are able not only to work together to improve the running of their classroom, but also to understand why this these routines are necessary.

Learning is deepened when emotions are engaged, so puppets can help in this process. If the children think they are representing a routine in order to help a forgetful bear, for example, there is a meaningful context and the children see the advantage in carrying out the activity. Puppets – and the characters you create for them – can provide real issues to address, and can help children to make connections with their own lives and experiences.

Helping Flip with routines

I used a teddy bear called Flip to establish routines and provide the children with a sense of independence, autonomy and control over their learning. Flip is a character who features in resources produced by Television Junction to strengthen home–school links. He came with a backpack containing a notebook and pencil, a toothbrush, and a letter from his mother, who lives on a ship. In the letter, Flip's mother explained that Flip could only draw ships and that she would love him to come to nursery to learn new things. She was clearly concerned for his development and needed help. The children looked after Flip, took turns to take him home for the night and learned about separation when he returned to his mother for Christmas.

By letting Flip stay in nursery, they were agreeing to work together to help him to learn. They showed him how to hang up his bag (on the peg – with his photo, that they insisted he needed) and how to sit at the computer. This gave the children the opportunity to rehearse all they had learned in nursery so far, and allowed the adults, through observation, to assess how the children had settled in. Once the children had got used to Flip, the next stage was to use him to develop and reinforce some essential nursery routines.

One morning I called the children together and announced that we had a problem in the nursery and needed their help. This immediately raised their interest and they relished the idea of helping me with a real problem. I showed them Flip, who had soggy, dripping paws and wet fur right up his arms. I explained that he had been trying to wash his hands, but clearly didn't know what to do. First, the children needed to agree that they could help Flip. This allowed us to state the problem and involve the children in the search for solutions. Through discussion we established some facts:

〉〉〉〉

- Flip needed our help.
- We knew how to wash our hands.
- We needed to show him how to do it.
- Flip sometimes forgets things, so we needed to provide something that could remind him when he forgot.
- He needed something he could look at and understand, because he gets jumbled with words.

The next problem facing the group was to decide how they could show him what to do in a way that he could understand, follow and refer to again. The children suggested that a picture would be a good idea, and through discussion decided that they might need more than one.

The children then had to work together to decide: what do we do when we wash our hands? We went through the process with actions, and I recorded their sequence on a whiteboard. With comments such as 'So far we've got … What do we do next?', the children were able to work collectively to finalize the sequence. They decided on appropriate action shots for the photographs, and over the course of the next few days I took the pictures with the children.

A set of annotated photographs of a child carrying out the routine was displayed in the toilet area. Green and red circles signified the start and end of the sequence and reinforced left-to-right orientation. Most importantly, above the sequence was a photo of Flip with the caption 'How do I wash my hands?' This put the learning into a context for the children and helped them to see the need for the routine. Flip couldn't wash his hands, and the sequence was the evidence of their attempt to help him. They had worked together to solve what was, to them, a real-life problem, and therefore the learning was contextual and relevant. The result was a routine devised and established by the children themselves that could be referred to whenever the inevitable slip-ups occurred.

Once the children had acknowledged that they were able to work together to help Flip, there was no stopping them. They relished the opportunity to help him whenever they could, and always rose to the challenge: 'Flip needs your help again!' Tackling other problems in this way helped to reinforce routines and properly establish a consistent approach, and the children came to understand the need for routine. Other problems included:

- How do we have snack?
- How do we use the book corner?

Use learning tools

The Critical Skills Programme provides a set of tools for teachers and children that support and facilitate the teaching and learning process. Some tools are aimed at the children (student tools), helping to guide them through processes such as decision making and collaboration. Some tools are used to support feedback and reflection (assessment tools) and other tools assist planning, enabling teachers to craft appropriate and meaningful challenges (coaching, planning, and design tools). As described below, when used in an early years setting alongside and as part of the development of a classroom community, these tools can greatly enhance learning. Sometimes the tool is modelled by the teacher and sometimes the children have the opportunity to use it within a group situation.

Brainstorming

An important element of community is the understanding that everyone can be heard, and that all opinions and ideas are valued. A brainstorm precedes the planning stages of a challenge. The activity allows everyone's ideas to be recorded effectively and efficiently – they can be distilled at a later stage. The children can then view the record of their ideas and refer back to it whenever they wish. As they refer back to it during the challenge, they will see the advantage of recording ideas.

Make a plan for your work

Working together towards common goals is a component of community, and planning activities together serves to bring the children together as a group. This can be modelled with the whole group before it is used by the children in their own

challenges. Children can sit together at a board with a 'To Do' list. They discuss what jobs need to be done and what activities they would like to undertake. The group agrees which ones are possible and they are recorded for all to see. For example, a To Do list might include:

☆ writing a thank you card to a special visitor

☆ collecting the dry leaves from the garden

☆ watering the plants in the classroom

☆ finishing a piece of work.

The children can see the big picture of what has to be done during the session, and understand who needs to do what and by when. It enhances the level of shared responsibility the children have for their environment, and provides a model which demonstrates that planning really can help you to get jobs done. As the children progress through the session, they come back together every so often to review

progress. At the end of the session (or sometimes part-way through) the children tick off what has been achieved. This information can be used in compiling the To Do list the following day.

Carousel

This tool builds community because it allows all ideas to be recognized and valued. It is a means of gathering lots of ideas in a short space of time, and also models writing for a purpose.

Split the children into three groups and have each group at a table with an adult. On each table is a large piece of paper and a coloured marker pen. At the top of the piece of paper is a question, to which the group have to supply as many answers as they can. Once ideas have been exhausted, each piece of paper is moved on to the next table and each group looks at another question. The adult reads out each answer recorded by the previous group, and if the group agrees, they can tick it. (Each group has a different coloured pen so it is clear which group the ideas and agreements belong to.) Additional responses are recorded, then the pieces of paper are moved on for the third and final time. This method means that the groups stay at their tables with their allocated adult throughout the activity. At the end, bring the whole class together to look at all the information collected.

Questions to consider could, for example, relate to a recent trip:

☆ What did you see at the optician's?

☆ What did you touch?

☆ What will we need to create our own optician's in the role-play area?

Or, questions might link to a particular book that the children have enjoyed, for example:

☆ What was your favourite page?

☆ How can you tell that (character) is sad/happy?

☆ How can you tell that it is night time?

The lists created quickly recap the trip and collate everyone's ideas. They can also provide a valuable reference to help with setting up a role-play area – modelling 'real' writing for a purpose. Always display the results of a carousel somewhere in the room. The children will enjoy looking back at them and showing their parents. See page 33 for an example of a carousel on ownership of role-play areas.

Thumb tool

An important aspect of a community is agreement on rules to ensure fairness. To understand this idea, the children need to experience decision making and the concept of consensus. The thumb tool is a quick and easy way for the children to answer a question or to show you how they feel. For us as teachers, it is an instant assessment tool that allows us to move the learning on accordingly. The children show a thumb up if they agree, a 'sideways' thumb if they have any reservations and a thumb down if they disagree. A child whose thumb is down can be invited to say why, which helps to develop reasoning skills. The thumb tool can be useful in a variety of situations, for example:

☆ Do you like playing with the new garage?

☆ Do you think there are enough cars?

☆ Would you like to go for a walk?

☆ Do you agree with (a character from a book)?

When children have been given this tool, they can use it when they need to get agreement within their challenge group.

What do I see happening?

In order to develop a collaborative learning community, it is important to observe the children at play in order to deepen your understanding of how they behave in a group situation. You will be able to see, for example, the leadership traits that are developing – who dominates? The process will also help you to identify which are likely to be successful pairings and groups for challenges. The following questions are useful for observing groups:

☆ Who talked?

☆ Who listened?

☆ Who shared ideas?

☆ Who asked questions?

Close observation of group activities will produce valuable information about individual characteristics and capabilities.

Move beyond a clapping culture

Establishing a clapping culture at the start of the year means that children begin to acknowledge the successes of their peers. They know what it feels like when their friends clap for them, and they enjoy celebrating together. This enhances the classroom community because children begin to feel that one person's success is a success for them too. This is the essence of a clapping culture.

However, the clapping can become a bit automatic, with little thought for the success being highlighted and praised. So as soon as the children have established a clapping culture, then it is time to move them on again. One way to do this is to encourage the children to comment upon success with phrases such as:

☺ I'm glad that Stacey got a sticker.

☺ I'm proud of Sebastian for getting the lunchtime sticker.

☺ That's good news, isn't it?

☺ Well done, Jake!

The children quickly pick up these phrases, and will start to use them as a matter of course. Children at this age often ask for stickers, especially when they see their peers being awarded them – and this strategy helps to move them away from this. A 'culture of competition' will not enhance your classroom community, as it is the exact opposite of everything you are trying to achieve through Critical Skills. By moving beyond the clapping culture, you are prompting the children to be truly pleased for their friends. At the same time, they are able to acknowledge that it is not their turn.

Helping children to celebrate their birthday is a great community builder. Children who have already had their birthday can remember what it was like to sit on the 'birthday cushion', and those yet to celebrate it can look forward to their turn. They share in the child's special day, and it serves to bring the group together.

Celebrating the success of the group of children who made jam tarts.

Introduce strategies for conflict resolution

This is one of the most important aspects of building a classroom community, purely because conflicts come up all the time. If the children are not equipped with the skills and strategies to deal with conflicts without adult intervention, then their ability to complete challenges will be severely compromised. The 6-step mediation process developed by the High/Scope Educational Research Foundation can be a useful method to help the children to resolve disputes:

Preparation, perspectives and strategies

- Acknowledge feelings.
- Gather information.
- Restate the problem.
- Ask for ideas for solutions and choose one together.
- Be prepared to give follow-up support.

(Evans, 2002)

First, make the sure the children acknowledge that there is a problem affecting their play. Encourage them to identify what the problem is and why it is a problem. If they cannot do this, then they will not be able to reach a solution. Then encourage the children to find solutions together, discussing whether or not they would work. Let them feel as though they are in control, choosing their own course of action and acting on their own ideas in order to solve their own problems. Always recap the situation so that the mediation process becomes explicit. Praise them when the situation has been resolved, and reinforce and celebrate the fact that they have solved the problem. The children could shake hands to signify that an agreement has been made and the conflict has been resolved. By being equipped with these skills, the children will be more able to deal with conflicts that arise when they are working in groups on challenges.

Value acts which promote community

For children to appreciate and value a quality – for example, kindness – they need to see and be reminded regularly that it is something you value. One way to do this is to record publicly instances of whatever it is that you want to promote.

The children can then share your appreciation, and the parents can also become involved. Eventually the children begin to recognize the quality and the behaviour, and the value is strengthened.

These children are developing their relationships with one another. The ability to turn take in conversation, to listen to others and to respond accordingly are prerequisites for group-work, and should be encouraged.

ideas in action

The Kindness tree

We introduced a 'Kindness tree', onto which we stuck leaves awarded for acts of kindness. Whenever a child showed kindness, we wrote down on a paper leaf what they had done. The leaves were then stuck onto the tree in a daily ceremony. This worked better than we had expected, because the children were very quickly able to verbalize what they needed to do in order to be kind – and therefore merit a leaf on the tree. Their comments included:

- 'We could share.'
- 'We could have kind hands.'
- 'We could say "please" at the snack table.'
- 'We could pass the milk.'

The children took this a step further by verbalizing what they had experienced or seen from other children. We had feedback such as:

- 'I asked William if I could play and he said, "Yes you can."'
- 'Macy helped me with my zip.'

Since we introduced the tree, the children have begun to solve issues without adult intervention. We hear comments such as:

- 'I think there is a problem.'
- 'Can I have a turn?'
- 'What could we do?'
- 'Shall we take turns?'
- 'We could share, couldn't we?'

The Kindness tree could be adapted to promote other values and behaviours. You could have, for example:

- A Sharing tree
- A Taking turns tree
- A Kind words tree
- A Happiness tree
- A Manners tree

*Examples
of leaves on the
Kindness tree*

Use whole-class and group check-ins

The notion of a 'check-in' is central to the Critical Skills model in the classroom. If learning is to be maximized, then the children need to feel safe emotionally. A check-in allows them the opportunity to share their thoughts with the group, gives the group an understanding of how everyone is feeling, and clears up any tensions which may otherwise affect subsequent activities. The basic idea is that the children come together and take part in a whole-group activity. The nature of the activity depends on the needs of the group. A check-in is part of the daily routine and can be requested by the children or adults at any time. It does not have a set time on a weekly timetable; the timing varies according to the needs of the groups and of individuals.

Children need to feel secure in the classroom environment before embarking on challenges. Give them opportunities for free-flow play, allow them to make bonds and connections, and let them be physically comfortable.

Below are some check-in activities that can be successfully implemented in a foundation stage setting. Again, this is not a completely new or original list, and in fact several of the check-in activities are similar to circle time games. There are endless ideas; these are just a few that I find work particularly well with young children.

Pass the smile

This is a simple activity that encourages the children to get eye contact with one another and develops their ability to take turns round a circle. One child smiles at the child sitting to their right, who smiles back. That child then passes the smile on by smiling at the child on their right. The smile makes its way silently around the whole circle. This is a great introduction to a group session, as it calms the children and gets them ready for focused work. Debrief by letting the children know exactly what they did to enable the activity to work: 'You needed to look at each other, work as a team and show good waiting. Thank you.'

Pass the clap

This activity runs along the same lines as Pass the smile, only this time the children take it in turns to pass a clap around the circle. Again, reinforce the need for children to look with their eyes, wait for their turn and help anyone who doesn't realize their turn has arrived. This strengthens the concept of teamwork, and the children should always celebrate their success. They can be challenged to see if they can pass the clap any faster or in the opposite direction.

Pass the frisbee

This is based on the same principles of building teamwork, collaboration, turn taking and a culture of success. Challenge the children to pass a frisbee round the circle as fast as they can – the need for speed really encourages a sense of team spirit.

Mexican wave

Another opportunity to develop teamwork. The children need to look at each other, watch and wait until it is their turn to pass on the wave. Apart from making teamwork explicit to them, it is a chance for you to see which children understand the concept of working with others.

Hello duck

Pass a small toy animal (we use a small yellow duck) around the circle, asking the children to each whisper their name into his ear. This is a good check-in to use at the start of the year when the children do not yet know each other very well and do not have the confidence to speak in front of the group. Encourage them to whisper their name and then pass the duck carefully on to the next child. The children have to wait for their turn, have the confidence to whisper to the duck, and understand that it needs to be passed on to the next child in the circle.

Good morning, good morning

The children sit in a circle. When it is their turn, each child says 'Good morning' to the child on each side of them. They then have the opportunity to share any news they may have. It is important the children know that the check-in is their opportunity to 'get things off their chest', because unacknowledged anxieties can impede progress in a challenge.

How do you feel today?

Talking about feelings is crucial in the challenge and group-work situation, and this is a simple way to get children to do this. Encourage the children to tell the duck how they feel today. They may choose to whisper, or to speak loud enough for the others to hear. As this check-in develops, the children will be able to expand on their expressions by explaining why they feel as they do, or by using a wider range of adjectives. Feeling 'happy' may become 'excited', 'proud' or even 'faberoonie'! Always articulate the meaning behind the activity. Explain that it important to let others know how we feel, so that if something is wrong, other people can try, as friends, to help.

What are you learning today?

As the children's confidence grows, check-in activities can be used to review a particular session or activity. Try always to articulate the learning intention behind a particular activity, for example: 'If you choose the puzzle, you will be learning to work together to make the whole picture.'

By giving the children regular opportunity to work together during a check-in, you are preparing them for challenges later on. Always tell them the skills that they are applying in order to carry out the activity, so that the learning is explicit. In addition, if the children know that there is something they want to share with the group, then a check-in will give them that opportunity. Use it as another strategy for resolving conflicts as they arise.

Encourage shared responsibility for the learning environment

The children need to know that this environment is their environment; that they have a shared, collective responsibility for it and a level of control over what happens in it. There are several strategies that can develop this sense of ownership. What we are aiming for here is for the children to feel comfortable in the setting and to want to maintain and improve it in an emotional and aesthetic way.

A task board

Have a 'task' board outside. The children look at the board every day to see what jobs need doing. These could be tasks such as watering the plants inside, weeding the flowerbeds, tidying the writing area, mopping around the water tray and sweeping the leaves. The children will learn that they are working together to make their classroom a better place in which to learn; they understand that it is their classroom, and therefore it is their responsibility to look after it.

Ownership over displays

Children can be involved in display work. They can be involved in selecting work to go up, help to position it, and enjoy watching as the staple gun attaches it to the wall. The work is theirs and they have ownership.

Ownership of role-play areas

There is a big emphasis on role play in early years settings – on re-creating roles and past experiences, and developing imaginary roles within a familiar setting. To keep this fresh, involve the children in the decisions, plans and preparation. The children can draw on their own interests to decide what the role-play area will be turned into. They can list resources they need, help to collect them, and then assemble the area as a focused activity. This avoids the potentially unsettling effect of arriving in the classroom on a Monday morning to be greeted by a new and unfamiliar role-play area. It also develops children's own interests and increases the chances of involving and interesting everyone.

For example, the children might visit a garden centre. On their return they could carousel (see page 26), recording what they saw, what they learned – and what resources would be needed in order to create 'our own garden centre'. Using the carousel method, the groups rotate until they have recorded their responses for all three questions. The list of resources becomes a powerful tool for learning, and engages the children in a purposeful activity. The children realize it is their responsibility to collect resources, often from home, and to set up the new role-play area. The items on the list get ticked off as they are added. As a result, the children know that the area belongs to them, and that it is their responsibility to use it appropriately and to keep it tidy – as would be the case in real life. The children enjoy working together; their pride in the product is obvious; and the process results in more meaningful and constructive play.

Seeing the big picture and sharing learning intentions

Another practice that helps to promote a collaborative learning environment is the sharing of learning intentions. If children are to maximize their learning, they need to be aware of what they are learning and why. Making learning intentions explicit to three and four year olds in a contextual and meaningful way is a challenge in itself – but it is possible. The learning intention for the week can be written up and explained at the beginning of the week. As the week goes on, children can collect evidence to show that they have fulfilled the intention. At the end of the week, they review their learning and decide whether they have achieved the recorded aims. A reward system could be introduced through the use of puppets – as illustrated below.

ideas in action

Harry and the apple tree

At nursery we have a small monkey named Harry. Harry's friends laugh at him because he doesn't like bananas (and everyone knows that this is what monkeys eat). This immediately strikes a chord with the children, and they instinctively want to help him. I explain to the children that Harry loves apples, and that they will need to work together to give Harry some apples. By now, the children are desperate to help him and agree that they will do whatever is necessary to ease Harry's plight.

Displayed on the wall is a tree with some red paper apples on it. On each apple I write a learning intention for the week, which I go through with the children. The number of learning intentions for the week varies, but usually two or three are achievable. A learning intention might be, for example: by the end of the week, you will have worked together to build a rocket. I tell the children, 'If you can do that, then we can give Harry the apple at the end of the week.' As the end of the week approaches, the children begin collecting their evidence – which is required in order for the apple to be picked. Comments such as 'I worked together with James and we shared the paintbrush' consolidate the learning for the children and emphasize the importance of collaboration.

At the end of the week, the children look back at the intentions and decide whether or not they have achieved them. If they agree that they have, and can offer examples or evidence as appropriate, then a child picks the apple and gives it to Harry. If the children decide that the learning intention has not been achieved yet, then the apple remains on the tree into the next week. In explaining what they have done, the children are reviewing their learning and

〉〉〉〉

making it explicit. They can then relate this to future learning experiences. In addition the children gain an overview – the big picture – of their learning.

The apple tree is also a way of celebrating success and reinforcing the idea that to achieve their goals the children need to work together. They clap when the apples are picked, in recognition of their collaboration and the extension of their learning.

Develop a Full Value Contract

A Full Value Contract (FVC) is essentially a set of agreed rules, compiled by children with adult support, that help the day-to-day running of the classroom go smoothly. The important difference between 'normal' rules and a Full Value Contract is that in the contract the rules are not imposed. The children decide what the rules should be in accordance with their experiences in and out of the classroom. They are more likely to adhere to them because they understand the advantages for themselves and others.

It is important that the expectations for behaviour and the general ethos of the setting are not your decision, but a joint decision between you and the children. This helps the children to take ownership and feel part of a collective learning environment. The FVC is a central part of the Critical Skills Programme and can be adapted to suit your children. Although the rules are agreed by the children, the FVC is based on three fundamental agreements:

> ☆ **We play hard and we work hard** – this relates to the effort put in by the children, setting the expectation that they will always try, and always have a go.

> ☆ **We play safe and we work safe** – this links to the safety aspect of nursery, setting the expectation that they will walk when inside, use gentle voices, and so on.

> ☆ **We play fair and we work fair** – this concerns the treatment of others and incorporates sharing and turn taking.

The introduction of the FVC should really come from the children. If they feel the need for some agreement in terms of rules and expectations, they will want to compile them. More importantly, if the children see the need for the contract then they are far more likely to adhere and refer to it.

Using Flip the bear to develop the FVC

I wanted to place the formulation of a Full Value Contract into some sort of context, so that the children would have a real purpose for constructing it. I showed the children a letter from Mother Bear, explaining that Flip had forgotten all the good things he had learned at nursery and asking if he could come back. He had forgotten good sitting and good listening, and she needed our help. As usual, the children were more than happy to help the wayward bear!

By now the children knew exactly what was expected of them, so they started thinking – what would they need to remind Flip about if he came back to nursery? They compiled a list and thought about how to show these things to Flip in a clear way. They were able to link this to the help they had given him the pevious term in the form of photographs showing him what to do. The children decided what would make good photographs, and through the course of one week set about posing for them. I displayed the photos on the registration board. (When the children arrive in the morning they take their photograph off their group board and place it on the registration board, where the contract is. In doing so, they are agreeing to abide by the contract. If a child forgets a particular part of the contract, I direct them to the photograph to remind them. This is a quick way for them to see what they should be doing without it becoming an issue, or disrupting their play.)

Our contract consisted of the following:

Work and play **safe**	Work and play **hard**	Work and play **fair**
We have gentle voices.	We try our best.	We have good waiting.
We walk in nursery.	We have a go.	We take turns.
We look after each other.		We work together.
We look after our things.		We say please and thank you.
We have good listening.		

We have gentle voices.   *We have good sitting.*   *We have good walking.*   *We have a go.*

Key points

★ Take every opportunity to emphasize the importance of working together to solve problems.

★ Help the children to realize that problems come along every day, and that they are able to solve them.

★ Try out some of the check-in activities, or use some of your own – you know your children and what they need.

★ Remember, your first aim is to establish the classroom community; only when you feel that it has been successful should you move on to a Critical Skills challenge.

Checklist

Use the following checklist to see whether your classroom community is sufficiently established to enable you to progress to the next stage.

☆ Do the children identify problems themselves?

☆ Are they able to resolve conflicts using strategies you have modelled?

☆ Is the daily routine established?

☆ Do the children refer to their Full Value Contract?

☆ Are the children able to work collaboratively when the opportunity is given to them by you?

By this stage your children should be beginning to work together to solve problems and make decisions. You should be able to detect signs of collaboration and a sense of 'community'. If this is the case, then you and your children might be ready to move towards a Critical Skills challenge. Remember, there is no fixed timescale for this and, as we know, all children are different. If you feel that there is still a great deal of conflict among your children and they still find working together difficult, then take things at a slower pace. The important thing is that you feel confident in your own ability and the abilities of your children. Spending more time developing the collaborative learning community will pay dividends in the end.

Chapter 3
A whole-class challenge

When early years practitioners hear the word 'challenge', it often conjures up images of something far too advanced for young children. The idea of children working in teams, solving problems and making 'products' all sounds too structured and adult-led. However, the approach taken in a Critical Skills challenge is one that can be used effectively with children of all ages.

A challenge starts with information for the children to find out, or a question for them to answer. A learning outcome is identified, along with a specific critical skill (e.g. creative thinking) and/or fundamental disposition (e.g, collaboration). From the skill or disposition, particular key attributes are selected – areas of that skill to be targeted during the process of the challenge. In addition, specific observable behaviours are chosen, and these are usually in the form of tools which will be used during the process. The criteria for assessment can be selected in terms of both the process and the product.

This is a very general outline of a challenge, and it can be broken down in accordance with developmentally appropriate practice for an early years classroom.

A Critical Skills challenge usually follows a Standard Teachers Operating Procedure (STOP) which, again, is adapted by every individual group. It does, however, provide a structure and sequence, as follows:

1. Create teams

2. Issue the challenge

3. 'Chunk' the challenge

4. Identify and define task roles

5. Establish criteria for:

    • product

    • desired outcome

    • process for collaborative work

6. Describe any special parameters.

Do not worry if you are not familiar with these stages. They may look rather daunting, but they are not all introduced simultaneously. In this and the next two chapters, we will look at how these processes can be introduced in an early years setting. And because ideas often become clearer in context, the 'Ideas in action' sections will illustrate how the processes were established in a real classroom.

The benefit of beginning with a whole-class challenge is that it provides the opportunity for you to model the operating procedure before the children carry out challenges in small groups. It may also be that your children develop their community and carry out mini problem-based challenges without ever getting to the stage where they work in small groups. If this is the case, then so be it. Every group of children is different, and only you will know what they are ready for.

When you feel that both you and the children are ready for a challenge, ask yourself the following questions:

☆ Have I observed collaboration in small-group situations?

☆ Is there evidence of conflict-resolution strategies being implemented independently?

☆ Is there evidence of children 'talking' as they work?

☆ Is the group able to offer workable solutions to daily problems that inevitably arise?

These particular indicators are suggested because they point to the elements of learning which facilitate the processes involved in a challenge. If you feel that the answer to these questions is 'yes', then your children might be ready for a whole-class challenge. If not, you could continue to develop and strengthen the classroom community, providing a suitable climate for learning. However, you may feel that despite not answering yes to all the above questions, your children are sufficiently equipped to deal with a challenge. It really comes down to professional judgement.

How to do a whole-class challenge

Introduce the problem

Start by introducing the problem, rather than the challenge. Some of the most effective challenges for the early years centre on a contextual problem. The advantage of this is that not only do the children need and want to solve the problem, but they have to work together in order to do it. The challenge therefore comes out of the problem, and the children construct and craft the challenge in the light of the problem they are faced with.

Chunk the challenge

Once the children have discussed the problem and decided on a workable solution, then together you make a plan and effectively 'chunk' the challenge. This means looking at stages of the process, what needs to be done, how it might be achieved and by whom. This models the process of 'chunking' in preparation for when the children work more independently.

Make a plan for the product

The next stage is to make a plan of the product. It is important that the children have some visual representation of what they are making, and this can be referred to throughout the process and amended if necessary. It also facilitates assessment, because when the product is complete it can be assessed against the intention and the criteria as outlined in the plan.

Allocate task roles

Task roles may be introduced (see page 62), although it may be better to defer this until subsequent challenges. The children are learning a new way of working, and too much can detract from the process focus. However, there might be opportunity to introduce roles in a contextual way – for example, the children might run out of time, which could lead to the idea of having a timekeeper.

Identify criteria for assessment

The children identify criteria for assessment in the following terms:

☆ You will need to …

☆ We are looking for …

The 'You will need to …' focuses on the process criteria of the challenge in terms of the product, what resources they have to use, what they have to make, what function it serves and so on. The 'We are looking for …' refers to the specific observable behaviours which will facilitate their work. These behaviours might be tools that the children have decided will help them to come to a decision or to record their ideas quickly.

Challenge sheet

To help introduce the challenge, you could use a challenge sheet. This is an important part of the challenge process, as it lays everything out in a clear way. From this, the children know what is expected from them and what you are looking for. By having this displayed prominently in the classroom, the group can refer back to it at various stages of the challenge. You could use the photocopiable challenge template on page 43 (making a copy from here or from the CD), or create one adapted to the needs of your class.

Work to make the product

It will probably be easiest to run the challenge over a number of days. For a challenge running over the course of a week, for example, an overview might look like this:

Monday	Introduce the problem; establish the challenge; chunk the challenge
Tuesday	Begin planning; produce a plan of the product for all to see and refer to
Wednesday	Work in small groups, with an adult coaching, on a component of the whole product

Thursday	Finish off with small groups; begin assembling the product
Friday	Finish assembling the product; test as appropriate; refer to plan; feedback and debrief

During the small-group times, invite children to suggest whom they would like to work with, and perhaps give them a team identity within the context of the larger group. Use this time to model decision-making strategies and encourage verbal communication, referring back to the plan to reinforce the importance of these as part of the process. Remind the children of what the challenge is, and of the specific observable behaviours that they agreed they would be able to demonstrate.

Debrief

When all the children have been involved in the process and the product is complete, take time to celebrate achievement. Use a variety of media to feed back. Make explicit exactly what they have achieved and what processes they have had to go through to get to the stage they have reached. Look at what worked well, and what could be improved for next time. This gives you a learning hook back into the cycle for the next challenge.

Ideas for whole-class challenges

Here are some examples of whole-class challenges which would facilitate the modelling necessary at this early stage. They are essentially problems that need to be solved together by the whole-class community:

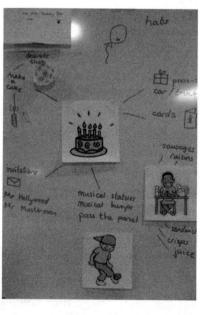

- ☆ Visitors can't find us; make some signs to show visitors how to find the classroom.

- ☆ This outside wall looks dull; brighten it up.

- ☆ We need to put this work somewhere important; change a display board.

- ☆ Build a home for a class puppet or toy.

- ☆ Now that we've visited the (garden centre, shop, doctor's surgery, etc.), we'd like to play in one. Change a role-play area.

- ☆ Make a giant birthday cushion to use for celebrating birthdays.

- ☆ Make a cake for a special occasion.

- ☆ Plan a party for someone special.

- ☆ Paint a giant picture to display in the hall.

- ☆ Tidy the nursery garden by weeding, collecting leaves, twigs, watering, raking and sweeping.

- ☆ Decorate a sheet to make a drape for open day.

- ☆ Help a visitor with a routine by taking photos to display.

- ☆ The outdoor toys are muddled up; sort them out.

- ☆ Build a bus to play in.

☆ THE CHALLENGE ☆ ☆ ☆ ☆ ☆ ☆

Chunk the challenge:

1 _____

_____

2 _____

_____

3 _____

_____

4 _____

_____

5 _____

_____

You will need to:

We are looking for:

Whole-class challenge – Build a monster

Following a term of community building, I felt the children were ready for their first structured challenge. I devised a problem-based challenge so that they would see the need to solve the problem and would engage in the process. Being aware that the children would need a lot of modelling, I began with a whole-class challenge.

The context of the challenge was Maurice Sendak's book *Where the Wild Things Are*. I had borrowed some small puppets of the monsters, but the children knew these would have to be returned. I steered the discussion towards the idea of making something that we could keep in nursery, and eventually the children decided on making a monster of our own.

The challenge sheet

I showed and explained the challenge sheet.

A monster challenge

I concentrated on the importance of teamwork, and in the debriefing focused on how they got the job done. This meant that the children would be in a stronger position when they undertook small-group challenges. By putting their hands up with ideas, they would be helping the group to select ideas and reach decisions. The children understood that they would all be contributing to the model in some way, and that everybody's part would be joined together. I wanted to reinforce the message that their individual efforts had combined to create the product.

☆ **THE CHALLENGE** ☆☆☆☆☆
Design, plan and make a model monster to sit on the chair in our class.
☆☆☆☆☆☆☆☆☆☆☆☆☆☆

Chunk the challenge:
1. Think about what monsters look like in *Where The Wild Things Are*.
2. Plan the monster so you know what you need. Lay out the model using the boxes.
3. Paint the monster. Join the pieces together.
4. Add on any other bits, like eyes.
5. _____

You will need to:
Put up your hand with your ideas, and then choose a part that you would like to help make.

We are looking for:
A finished monster
Children who take turns

Critical Skills in the Early Years © Vicki Charlesworth (Network Educational Press, 2005)

The plan

I stressed the importance of having a plan, especially as they were making a single collaboratively constructed monster. I suggested that they might like to draw him first, so they wouldn't forget what they had decided, and the children agreed.

We placed the drawn plan in a prominent place so that it could be referred to during the construction. The next stage was choosing shapes for the parts of his body. For this, the children sat in a circle and I placed one box in the middle that would become the 'trunk'. Then the children selected different shaped boxes for other parts, asking others if they agreed. One child stood up so we could measure his leg, because the children wanted their monster to stand as tall as they were.

Reinforcing expected behaviour and highlighting 'What I am looking for'

Throughout this process, I was reinforcing the importance of consulting each other, making decisions and listening. If somebody put their hand up and said, 'What we could do is …', then I would say, 'Children, did you notice what Fraser did? He put up his hand because he had an idea, and he waited for his turn. He has been listening and he has another idea. Well done, Fraser, I'm really proud of you.' This level of reinforcement and acknowledgement is necessary with children of this age, especially in the early stages of challenges, when they are still learning what is expected of them. Once the body had been constructed, the children looked back at their plan and chose parts that they would like to be responsible for.

In small groups, the children worked collaboratively to paint the body parts.

A 'problem' to overcome

I instigated a problem: the eyes wouldn't stick. This forced the children to go back to the plan together and think again. Luckily, our headteacher is a former DT adviser so we recruited him to help us. This was problem solving at its best, and the children could see the value of drawing on an 'expert' to assist them in their common goal.

Feedback through anecdotal notes

With older children you could give suggestions by leaving a post-it note on a desk, for example, but it is more difficult to give feedback during a challenge when the children are unable to read your comments. I used a puppet called Hedley, who likes watching the children in nursery. As the children were working, they knew that Hedley was watching from his spot on the shelf. Occasionally I would approach him for a comment. The children were willing to accept Hedley's opinions and acted on them if necessary. (For more on feedback, see Chapter 6.)

The debrief

The children sat on the rug in front of their finished monster and next to their plan, and gave themselves a clap. They were certainly proud of their product. I had taken photos of all the stages of the challenge and annotated these in a book.

As part of the debrief, I read the book to the children as a way of recapping all that they had done to get to this stage. I reminded them that I had been looking for children who took turns, and asked them to tell me if they could remember doing this. Although some of them could, it was more powerful to

use Hedley, the puppet. I used him to relay my notes about those who had passed the paint, those who had waited for their turn and those who said, 'Your turn now.' This reminded the children and they were justly proud of their collaboration.

They were able to spot things missing from the plan, so I suggested that next time we look back at our plan more carefully. I also asked them what they had particularly liked, and then what they thought they would like to do next time. I prompted them by saying that they couldn't take the monster home because he belonged to everyone, so maybe next time they would like to make one each.

Finally, the children gave themselves another clap as we looked back at the challenge sheet to see that we had achieved everything: they had taken turns and there was a finished monster on the chair.

Moving on from the debrief

The whole-class challenge exposes the children to the following concepts:

☆ They can work together to produce a shared product.

☆ They can make a plan so they know what needs to be done.

☆ They need to listen to each other.

☆ They need to make decisions to get things done.

The children knew that the monster didn't look exactly the same as the plan because they had forgotten to look back at it. The plan was there to help them remember what they needed, but they had not referred to it. This was clear to the children in a visual way because the monster had horns and a tail on the plan but these were missing from the model. This really set the context for the next challenge. In addition, the children had commented that they couldn't take the monster home because he was too big and he belonged to everyone. We discussed the possibility of making something each next time. However, this provided me with the opportunity to remind the children that working together can really help them. We decided that a challenge in pairs would be the way forward.

This is a crucial element of the Critical Skills Programme. Assessing learning at the end of a challenge really does provide the children with an understanding of the process of learning (what they did, how it helped them and what would be needed next time). For learning to be maximized, it needs to build on experience. This is essentially what Critical Skills does. It provides the opportunity to emphasize the importance of building on previous learning. It develops the idea of deciding what has worked well, refining it and moving learning forwards. This is meta-cognition at an advanced level: the children can see what they need to achieve in order to further their learning and are able to act on this with their next challenge.

Common problem

It can be difficult to avoid taking the modelling too far and taking over. You may find yourself making decisions for the children, giving them the impression that all decisions lie with you.

Possible solution

Be aware of this and know why it should be avoided. The children need to feel as though they are in control; let them decide the course of action throughout the challenge. The concepts of ownership and responsibility, and an understanding of cause and effect, and decision making are all fundamental to the Critical Skills Programme. The children need to experience these skills for themselves in order to develop them. In addition, they need to experience success and to understand that this is a direct result of their own decisions and their own actions. Remember, they should be debriefing their own challenge and not yours!

Key points

★ Be confident that the children have the skills necessary to approach a challenge before you begin. Go back to Chapter 2 and work on developing the classroom community if you are not sure.

★ Remember, challenges are only one part of the Critical Skills Programme. Take things slowly and carry out only what your children (and you) are ready for.

★ Work as a whole class to facilitate the modelling of the process.

★ Choose one skill, such as working together, which will benefit the children in future challenges. You may need to break this down further into smaller chunks, such as taking turns, listening, and so on.

★ The debrief is the most important part of the challenge. Make it clear to the children exactly what they did, what they learned and how this will impact on what they do next time.

Chapter 4
Challenges in pairs and small groups

The whole-class challenge works in a number of ways. It introduces the children to problem-based collaborative learning, giving them an opportunity to work through the process – from discussion to planning to making – on a shared product. It facilitates the processes of feedback and assessment, further strengthening the learning that the children have experienced. The modelling also allows children to become familiar with learning tools, as and when it is appropriate for them to use them.

A small-group challenge involves more modelling but in a less intrusive way, thus allowing the children to experiment with the challenge scenario more independently. The key difference is in terms of the product. Rather than producing a single whole-class collaborative product, there is one product per small group. It is probably best to start off in pairs for the following reasons. Firstly, the children will have to make decisions, and this is easier to negotiate when you have to consider only one other person's point of view. Secondly, the act of listening is a complex one and in some cases needs to be taught; this is more achievable in a pair situation. Thirdly, the children complete a planning sheet, and this will need some adult direction in the first instance. From the teacher perspective, a group of two allows you to tune into the children easily and gives you the opportunity to coach individuals without the added pressure of lots of other children. The method and example given below therefore describe a pairs challenge, but the suggestions apply equally to challenges in small groups of more than two.

How to do a small-group challenge

Introduce the problem

Introduce the challenge in a similar way, in terms of a problem that needs solving. This discussion should still be carried out with the whole group. Consider workable and unworkable options, and use appropriate tools to help the children reach an agreement on the course of action. Use photographs, drawings, pictures and words to formulate the challenge, and record it using a challenge sheet. This will be referred to throughout the challenge process, but there is no advantage in making this wordy. The following headings will suffice:

☆ The challenge (the problem which needs solving)

☆ You will need to … (chunking of the challenge into doable sections)

☆ We are looking for … (the specific observable behaviours and skills).

Let each child decide on a partner they would like to work with. Whom they choose will tell you a lot about them: some children choose someone they enjoy playing with; others choose someone they perceive to be 'good' at painting or drawing or some other activity; others will simply choose the first child they see when asked (and whose name they know). All of this information will help as you assess the children, not only in this challenge but in others to come.

Make a plan for the product

Once the challenge has been introduced to the whole group, then the planning moves to paired work. This is a focused activity and needs adult support. For some children it can be helpful to give them a 'now or later' option, depending on their level of engagement in other areas of the room. If children are highly engaged in their current activity it may not be productive to call them away at this moment. Offer them the option of planning their product a bit later in the session, making it clear to them that they will do it later, and giving them time to prepare for this. When a pair is ready to start, go through the challenge again to clarify and refresh the problem, then invite them to talk to each other. This can be the stage requiring the most intervention. Some children have their own idea of a product and find it extremely difficult to understand that the product is to be shared and that there will not be one each. Persevere and offer support where necessary.

Planning sheet

It may be helpful to use a planning sheet, such as the one on page 52. It is important to introduce this in context and in relation to previous experience. In the whole-class challenge, the children completed a plan and referred back to it to remind them of what they needed to do next – it helped them with the process. This time, they will need a plan to follow in case they forget what the product is going to look like or what they will need to make it. The children write their names and draw a picture of what they want their product to look like. They may like to stick pieces on to their plan to remind them of resources they will need, and it can be annotated if they wish. Although the supporting adult can annotate, the emphasis is on the children's own work.

Work to make the product

Once the plan is complete, the children are ready to make the product. This may be done in another session – perhaps the next day – in order to maintain concentration and focus. By stopping and restarting the next day, interest is refuelled and the process continues, often at a deeper level. The level of intervention required here really depends on the individual children. Some are good verbal communicators and can articulate ideas, offer suggestions and even ask for ideas from their partner. Others will need prompting to re-establish the problem and say where they are up to in the process, and to move the process on. The important thing to remember is that it is the processes that are important, not the finished product. If the target skill was communication, for example, you would be looking to see if the children:

☆ turned to face each other

☆ listened to what each other had to say

☆ responded appropriately

☆ offered suggestions.

You could ask another member of staff to take photographs as the children are working through the planning and making stages of the challenge. You can then print these as thumbnails and attach them to the plan. This will help you to highlight the process during the feedback and assessment session.

Debrief

Once the products are complete, the feedback and debrief session can begin. Highlight the processes, explaining – perhaps with the aid of photographs – what you saw happening. Take every opportunity to value the processes with the children, so that they begin to see them as important too. Debrief by identifying what worked well and what could be done differently next time. To begin with, the children will tend to focus on the product rather than the process: they might say 'The red paint looks nice' rather than 'We had a good idea – to use red'. Having more than one product means that the children have the opportunity to peer-assess as well as self-assess; again take this as far as you feel is appropriate with your children. The most important thing to remember is to celebrate success and what the children have achieved.

Ideas for challenges in pairs

☆ Paint an animal for a collaborative display.

☆ Depict the class's favourite activity for a display.

☆ Build a rocket, ship, car or other mode of transport for a class pet (using junk).

☆ Make salt-dough figures for a class fort, pirate ship, farm or train set.

☆ Make a Lego house for a particular classroom character, such as a puppet.

☆ Choose and draw a favourite book for the walls of the book corner.

☆ Work together on a collage to add to a whole-class montage.

☆ Weave material through fencing to brighten up the outside area.

☆ Use natural objects such as pine cones and twigs to make a piece of art on the grass outside.

☆ Make a clay animal for a class zoo.

☆ Plan snacks for the week, listing food to buy.

Planning sheet

Names	
Our plan	**What we need**

Pairs challenge – build a rocket

After reading Tony Ross's *Michael*, a book about a boy who builds a rocket, I challenged the children to build a rocket to take Michael into space. The challenge looked like this:

Making a plan

Each pair made a plan so they knew what they would need and what their rocket would look like.

What am I looking for?

When discussing the challenge sheet at the beginning, I told the class that I was looking for children who could work together. I wanted them to really understand what they would need to do and display if they were to meet this criterion, and they were able to suggest things like taking turns and listening.

I showed the children photographs of themselves working in the nursery.

☆ **THE CHALLENGE** ☆ ☆ ☆ ☆ ☆
☆ *With a friend, plan and make a*
☆ *rocket to take Michael into space.*
☆ ☆ ☆ ☆ ☆ ☆ ☆ ☆ ☆ ☆ ☆ ☆ ☆

Chunk the challenge:

1 *Choose a friend to work with.*

2 *Think about what rockets look like in Michael and in other books.*

3 *Plan the rocket so you know what you need.*

4 *Make your rocket.*

5 *Paint the rocket.*

You will need to:
Put up your hand with your ideas and listen to your friend.

We are looking for:
A finished rocket that can carry Michael
Children who work together

Critical Skills in the Early Years © Vicki Charlesworth (Network Educational Press, 2005)

I asked them to tell me which ones showed children working together – and if the children were not working together, how could they tell? This proved a powerful activity because it was so visual, and allowed the children to justify their opinions. It reinforced the idea of 'working together', increasing their chances of achieving this during the challenge.

The planning sheet

They children were going to make only one plan per pair, so they had to work together to do this successfully. The planning sheet had space for their names, a sketch of their intended rocket, and a list of things they would need. They sat with a nursery officer who was able to assist where necessary, but she had been briefed to intervene only where necessary. We encouraged the children to rummage through the junk modelling materials and select what they would like to use. We also encouraged them to consider joining techniques, and

》》》》

displayed various methods for them to choose from. These included split pins, masking tape, Sellotape, Blu-tack®, glue, treasury tags, staples and paper clips. We suggested that they stick sample materials to their plan, so that when they came to make the rocket they would remember what to collect. Adults helped to annotate the descriptions, although we encouraged contextual, 'real' writing from the children.

Moving on from the planning stage

As pairs completed their plans, they were ready to construct their rocket. By referring back to their plan they were able to choose suitable 'junk' pieces, attach them in a variety of ways, and paint and decorate them as they wished. I used the puppet Hedley again to offer suggestions and to highlight collaboration and teamwork. The children seemed more able to take constructive comments and suggestions from Hedley than from me, possibly because emotions were engaged. Throughout the construction stage, I took photos, in preparation for the debrief, of children taking turns, working together, agreeing and enjoying their challenge.

The debrief

During the debrief, I shared the book of photographs depicting stages of the challenge, and asked Hedley for his observations. One such observation was of two children who shook hands when they reached a decision. The children were invited out to the front to show the others what they had done, and the others

ideas in **action**

clapped because it proved that they were 'working together'.

The debrief showed higher-level thinking as the children were able to draw upon their experiences and link this to future learning. They had built on from last time by planning and then following the plan throughout the challenge. The pairs had worked together to make a product – and the class decided that next time they could make one large collaborative rocket.

The model rockets were hung from the ceiling, and in the subsequent days and weeks the children pointed to their models, talked to their

The debrief showed that the children were focusing on product rather than process. I was confident that, through more modelling, this deeper thinking would come.

Rocket Challenge

Worked Well ☺	Next Time
Painting the rocket	A different shape (a box one)
Glueing it together	A splatter rocket
Putting the engine on	One big rocket altogether
Working with a friend	

parents about them, and chose their favourite ones. One child suggested testing them out to see if Michael would fit, and we discussed whether we should have done this. This provided the opportunity to further their learning by crafting a challenge which would include a testing section.

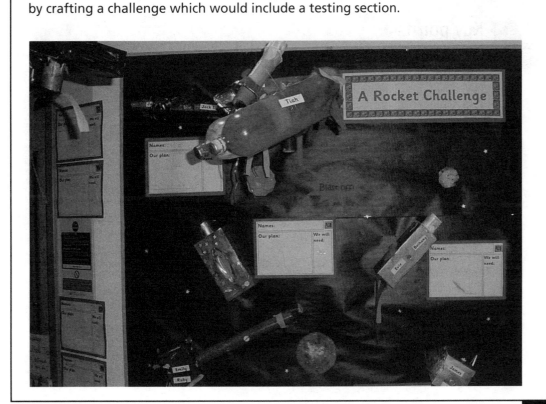

Common problem

Looking at challenges in isolation and planning them as individual activities may become a problem. You will need to be fairly flexible with your planning. Although the knowledge-based content can be decided in advance, it is a mistake to decide upon the skills to be developed.

Possible solution

Use the debrief to plan the focus for the next challenge. This means the children can begin to reflect upon their learning and see how this affects what comes next. Let them know that you are helping them with the things they need help with.

Common problem

When the children work on a challenge in pairs, the problem of whom the product belongs to can be a problem for some children when it comes to the 'taking-home' time.

Possible solution

Make it clear that the children are working on a problem that will help everyone. They can be helped to understand that their product actually belongs to the whole group, as part of a whole-group collaboration.

Key points

★ Build on from the debrief of the previous challenge so that the children can see how their reflection can develop their learning.

★ Don't worry if the debrief focuses on product rather than process: as the children get more used to reflection, they will be better equipped to consider the process.

★ Encourage the children to complete the planning sheet in pairs. This builds on from the whole-class plan and introduces the children to a valuable learning tool.

Chapter 5

A sequence of challenges and the introduction of roles

Children deepen their understanding by playing, talking, observing, planning, questioning, experimenting, testing, repeating, reflecting and responding to adults and to each other.

DfEE (2000) *Curriculum Guidance for the Foundation Stage* (QCA)

One of the fundamental components of the Critical Skills Programme is the concept of learning as a cycle.

Children engage in the learning, perform the task required as a solution to the problem and reflect on their achievements. The concept of a learning cycle becomes clear in reality when children connect their achievements to what happens next in terms of their learning – they are utilizing their understanding in order to take their learning to a higher level. This model epitomizes how young children learn, and reflects the process described in the Curriculum Guidance document and in formative assessment research.

When anyone is trying to learn, feedback about the effort has three elements:

Recognition of the desired goal, evidence about present position, and some understanding of a way to close the gap.

All three must be understood to some degree by anyone before he or she can take action to improve learning.

Black and Wiliam (1998)

The Critical Skills Programme offers the teacher a highly effective way of leading children through this process, that allows them to take control of their own learning. So, to recap on the process so far, the stages in developing a Critical Skills early years classroom are as follows:

☆ Time is spent developing the classroom community before embarking on challenges.

☆ A whole-class challenge is introduced as a problem which the children need to solve together. This includes modelling of the processes involved, such as brainstorming and sharing ideas, planning, decision making and debriefing.

☆ Following on from the debrief, another challenge is formulated. The new challenge builds on what has been learned in the previous one. Thus, the learning cycle is modelled and made explicit to the children

☆ The cycle is repeated through more challenges.

A sequence of challenges

The following Ideas in action section describes a sequence of challenges, showing how each debrief affects the focus of the next challenge.

Small-group challenge – make a bird scarer

The outcome of the rocket challenge was that the children wanted to make 'one big rocket' with everyone helping. I explained that the disadvantage of this was that we would have only one product shared between everyone. The compromise I suggested was to work in a group of four. They would be able to use more people – enhancing the quality input into the product – and would be making more than one product.

This idea tied in with their next challenge. I explained that the planters outside were being pecked by birds. The previous week, the children had spent time planting geraniums, so the matter was of clear concern. They wanted to make something that would scare the birds away. Because there were two large planters, making one bird scarer would not be enough. We decided that three scarers in each planter would be needed to frighten away any birds. So I suggested the children should work in seven groups of four – making a total of seven products.

We talked together about features of bird scarers. This led the children to think about aspects such as colour and texture, which facilitated the planning stages as they moved into small groups.

Selecting groups

The priority here was that the children felt secure in their groups, so I let the children group themselves according to friendship. Some of the children were not at the stage where they could acknowledge who their friends were, but could say which children they would like to work with.

〉〉〉〉

ideas in action

The context

The children knew that they needed to work together, and that the product was to be a scarer to frighten the birds away from their flowers. The challenge sheet highlighted what we were looking for (good listening), and the children were keen to know what this was. By now, they knew that Hedley would be looking out to see who was doing or saying what, and they liked to know from the start what they would need to do.

The outcome

The children completed and followed a plan to make a bird scarer. Good listening was an appropriate aspect of problem solving to choose because it was challenging for the children to work in groups of four. The photographs of the challenge showed some groups working without one of their members, and often this child appeared to be struggling for a role.

These images proved to be very powerful in demonstrating teamwork, and how it feels to be included or left out. From this I helped the children to reach the decision that the next challenge should be back in pairs, to facilitate working together.

Pairs challenge – create a world of colour

The children had worked together to paint a 'world of colour', which was displayed in the nursery. They had mixed colours to extend from small colour prints, each of which was stuck in the middle of a piece of A2 card. The prints were of work by John Dyer, the artist in residence at the Eden Project. Once the pieces of card were joined together, we decided they looked like a 'world of colour'. I introduced the 'problem' by suggesting that it looked a bit bare and that they could help me to make it look more interesting. We talked about the usual (glitter!) before one child suggested that animals would look good in the world. We talked about whether they should be easily seen or not, and thought it would be good to try hiding them.

〉〉〉〉

ideas in **action**

The context

The children knew that they would be working in pairs. I told them that I would be looking for children who worked together. We discussed listening, making a decision, sharing and taking turns. They knew that Hedley would be watching.

The outcome

The children worked in pairs to complete and follow a plan to create collage animals for the collaborative 'world of colour'. One pair had difficulty deciding which animal to make. (One wanted a giraffe; the other an elephant.) They were unable to see that without a decision they could not progress and make the animal. I reminded them that they had to work together on the *same* animal. This was a good opportunity to model the process of decision making, and the children eventually shook hands to signify that a decision had been reached.

During the debrief, I highlighted the importance of decision making by drawing attention to those pairs who were able to do it. Some children were confident enough to come to the front and talk through the process for the others, articulating why they decided to make the animal they had. We compared their plans to their finished products. We decided that next time we would continue to build on decision making. The children had worked well in pairs and thought that they might be ready for a challenge in groups of three.

Small-group challenge – a boat for Harry

In our nursery we have a small monkey called Harry. One day I stopped the children and told them that there was a problem. Harry was all wet. They immediately went to find a towel for him and began to speculate about what could have happened. Eventually Harry, who was extremely shaken, told them that he had wanted to cross the water tray but he had fallen in. This established the problem and introduced the challenge: the children needed to help Harry to get across the water. They suggested bridges and cars, but we eventually decided a boat would be the safest method.

〉〉〉〉

The context

This time the children would work in groups of three. They knew that they needed to shake hands when they had made a decision and that we would be looking for groups who worked together.

The outcome

By now the children could identify others with whom they worked well, and this facilitated the establishment of groups. The planning was no problem, and because it was the summer term, many could not only write their name but had the confidence to annotate their drawing with the materials they would need. We had a testing session, and if the boat floated they could put Harry in it to see if it was strong enough. Harry was frightened at first, having had flashbacks of his previous soaking, but the children proved what good friends they are and gave him a cuddle first.

The learning cycle

In the sequence of challenges described above, the children were able to identify the aspects which needed strengthening by constantly reflecting on their learning. Each challenge led on from the previous debrief, giving them the opportunity to consolidate an area which they felt would help them to work together. Because the children were aware of the process throughout, their learning was deepened.

The sequence in fact began with the challenges described in Chapters 3 and 4. The summary below shows all the challenges in context and how the focus for each was identified from the learning of the children.

Challenge	Outcome	Next focus
Monster	We didn't look back at the plan.	Write a plan in pairs.
Rocket	We could make a better product with more people.	Working in a group of four.
Bird scarer	A group of four was too big.	Working together in pairs.
World of colour	Sometimes we need to decide together.	Making decisions.
A boat for Harry	We work best in threes – could we have jobs to do?	Introduce task roles.

Ideas for small-group challenges

☆ Make windmills for outside.

☆ Plan, buy and plant bulbs for spring.

☆ Plan, buy and prepare a snack for the class.

☆ Make a film to show parents what happens in class, selecting parts of the day to depict.

☆ Build a car for a class pet.

☆ Decorate a chair for the child with a birthday.

☆ Make biscuits for the class.

☆ Take pictures to depict a class routine.

☆ Take pictures for a rubric-style progression of observable behaviours (see p.69).

For more ideas for challenges, see the challenge bank in the community section of the Critical Skills website.

Introducing task roles

Once the children are comfortable working in a group situation, then you may consider introducing task roles. Before you do this, ask yourself the following questions in relation to the small-group experiences your children have had so far:

☆ Do the children engage in the task?

☆ Do they show signs of respecting the opinions and views of their peers?

☆ Are they willing to take instruction from a particular member of the group?

If the answers are all 'yes', then the chances are the children will benefit from moving to the next level. Even if the answers are 'no', now might still be a good time to introduce some of the task roles in an attempt to motivate and engage the children. Again this is a matter of professional judgement.

Task roles help to keep the children focused, ensure the product is finished in the time allowed, and offer everyone a chance to be included. Task roles in groups are commonly as follows:

☆ **Facilitator** – reminds the team about the job in hand; suggests tools to use

☆ **Recorder** – makes notes on behalf of the group

☆ **Timekeeper** – keeps the group up to date on how much time they have to complete the challenge

☆ **Materials manager** – responsible for collecting materials from shared areas

☆ **Quality checker** – compares the quality of the product in terms of the criteria established in the planning stages

☆ **Team representative** – feeds back to the rest of the class, and the teacher, on behalf of the group

Not all these roles are appropriate for young children, although most can be modified and adapted to suit their needs. A good strategy is to introduce one role per challenge, so that the children gradually become familiar with them and can distinguish them easily. Take a look at what your children have achieved so far and choose a role that they would benefit from immediately. The roles can be translated into simpler terms:

☆ **Facilitator** – has the last decision if the group cannot agree

☆ **Recorder** – makes a list of what the group need

☆ **Timekeeper** – has a sand timer or stopwatch to remind the group about the time

☆ **Materials manager** – responsible for getting everyone a pencil or painting apron, for example

☆ **Quality checker** – holds the plan and is prompted to look back at this

☆ **Team rep.** – when called, tells the teacher and the other children what the group have been working on

The children could devise badges with suitable photographs to depict and distinguish each role.

Task roles

One morning I told the children that I had not had time to get the snack shopping, and that I needed their help. Their challenge was to provide a healthy snack for everyone in nursery. They would work in small groups and take turns to get the snack ready each day through the week. They would have to:

1 decide what their snack would be
2 make a shopping list
3 go to the shops to buy everything
4 prepare the snack
5 serve it at the usual snack time.

To facilitate the process, I suggested jobs to ensure everything got done, while they decided who would do what. The jobs were:

• **Timekeeper** – we set the oven timer at several intervals during the challenge, and it was the timekeeper's job to remind the group
• **Recorder** – wrote the shopping list
• **Reporter** – responsible for reading the list out to the whole group, announcing what the snack would be for that day
• **Quality checker** – decided which fruit was the best to buy, and tasted the snack when it was ready to see if it was good enough

We did not make use of the facilitator role, as I felt this was not concrete enough for the children.

Common problem

The risk in doing a small-group challenge with young children is that not everyone 'buys in', and that one child is uninvolved throughout.

Possible solution

Make the problem explicit to the group. The 'I think there is a problem here' route may prove fruitful. However, it may need to wait until the debrief before the others in the group – and even the child concerned – become aware of the situation. It is only then that you can plan to avoid this in the future. Where possible, help the children to allocate specific roles. In my experience, groups of three have proved more productive than groups of four.

Key points

★ Make the sequence explicit to the children: 'Last time you decided … so this time we need to …'

★ Keep some constants, for example always use the same planning sheet, and debrief in the same way. This allows the children to focus on what is important for the particular challenge, without being distracted by too many variables.

Chapter 6
Feedback and assessment

The benefits of formative assessment in the early years

The Critical Skills experiential cycle of learning includes a stage of reflection, which facilitates the next connection. In other words, children need to assess their achievements and their learning in order to take their learning to the next level through subsequent challenges. Throughout this book there are examples of challenges which result in further learning experiences, facilitated by *formative* assessment strategies. This chapter will deal with these strategies in detail.

Formative assessment is a tool for promoting children's learning. It helps us, as teachers, to identify where the children are, and highlights the next step for our teaching and the children's learning. When the information from assessment is used as feedback to adapt the teaching work to meet learning needs, it becomes formative. Essentially, the learning is determined by the learner, in a process of identifying what is needed next. In the words of Shirley Clarke (2001),

> If we think of our children as plants ... summative assessment of the plants is the process of simply measuring them. The measurements might be interesting to compare and analyse, but, in themselves, they do not affect the growth of the plants. Formative assessment, on the other hand, is the garden equivalent of feeding and watering plants – directly affecting their growth.

There are several strategies used to formatively assess the progress, achievements and learning of young children, and I will outline these in general terms before applying them to the experiences in our own setting.

☆ **Feedback** – this is where the teacher comments on the learning process as it is happening and when it has finished. This includes comments such as, 'I noticed that you ...', 'I liked the way you ...', 'You are (verbalize what the child is doing/saying) ... what a good idea! This helps because ...'

☆ **Self-assessment** – this is where children are encouraged not only to comment on their process and product learning, but to critically assess it at the same time. The use of stickers (e.g. What I think, How I feel) to assess products is one strategy to use in the early stages, as this gives children the experience of feeding back and commenting on their own achievements. This can be developed to the point where children discuss with you ways to improve their work. This discussion can be general or specific, depending on the skill or disposition being focused on in the challenge.

☆ **Peer-assessment** – this stage is perhaps the most advanced, as it requires children to look beyond their own achievements and be critical of the work of the other children in the group. 'Two stars and a wish' can be a useful strategy here. The child with the product explains the process and the end product to his peers. That child then chooses two peers to each offer one positive comment concerning either the product or the process – two 'stars'. The child then looks to another peer who is willing to offer a 'wish': an element that could be improved next time. Clearly, it is difficult for the children to comment on the process unless they have been involved in some way, or have heard feedback in relation to it.

These strategies are all employed during a debrief session, which is when the next learning step is identified and agreed by the whole group.

The advantages of formative assessment are well documented (Black and Wiliam, 1998) and it has a fundamental place in an early years classroom. We aim to create a safe learning environment and a climate of trust in our settings, and these formative assessment methods can help in developing this. If the learning is explicit and the children begin to assess this themselves, then a shared responsibility for learning begins to emerge. This is enhanced when the children are able to assess each other's learning (peer assessment). By planning opportunities for the use of formative assessment strategies, teachers can maximize learning in the classroom and create a culture of learning that is truly powerful.

Links to early learning goals

As early years practitioners, we are constantly observing our children in terms of the stepping stones and early learning goals laid out in the Curriculum Guidance document (2000). When working in a Critical Skills classroom, we are also observing and assessing children against the Critical Skills and fundamental dispositions.

When observing a Critical Skills challenge, we have a particular skill at the forefront of our minds, be it problem solving, decision making or creative thinking. However, in observing the critical skills, we are also observing children's abilities as outlined in the stepping stones and early learning goals. (The relationship between Critical Skills and ELGs is set out in detail in the next chapter.) This doubling up means that incidental observations towards ELGs can still happen in a Critical Skills classroom.

Feedback

There are several ways to feed back that will help children identify where they are in terms of learning and where they need to go next. The process enables the children to consider how they are going to take the learning on and means that a new focus can be established.

Using post-its

One feedback tool is to pass the children post-it notes so that individuals can receive a comment without the group being disturbed. Clearly, written comments will not always be appropriate, but you could develop a system of symbols which the children become familiar with. A smiley face, for example, might mean 'you are working well' and a 'thumbs up' might signify 'you are offering good ideas'.

Using oral feedback

Perhaps the feedback tool most commonly used in the early years is oral feedback where the teacher comments on the process or product directly to the child involved, and at an appropriate moment so as to maximize learning. The timing aspect is crucial, because in five minutes' time the focus for that child may have changed. In order to do this, the teacher needs to be working directly with the child, observing and coaching, so as to identify the moments worth feeding back on.

When feeding back to children during a session, it is important to make expectations of quality explicit. Comments such as, 'I liked the way you …' and 'I saw you …' provide instant, contextual feedback as children are working, and are a powerful way to enhance future learning. We have found it beneficial to tell children what we're looking for as they are working, with comments such as, 'I am looking for someone who can take turns' and 'I wonder if I'm going to spot someone who can sort the buttons?' This helps the children to focus on what you are looking for, and they are reminded of this as you feed back to others.

Sometimes feedback is more appropriate at the end, usually when summarizing the whole process in the light of the finished product. As well as offering support and encouragement, oral teacher feedback helps the child to identify their own achievements, as they are modelled through the feedback.

Using puppets

Having a puppet who watches the children as they work can be a great way of engaging children in their learning, because the puppet can be 'looking' for specific observable behaviours and can focus on the skill being developed. The puppet can feed back at the end of the session to tell children what he or she has seen and heard during the course of the challenge.

Using photographs

The use of photographs is a most effective and powerful method of giving feedback to young children and helping them to assess themselves. They can observe and interpret what is happening in the picture or film, no text is required, and they can see the feedback in context. A photograph provides an instant record of a particular teaching or learning moment, which may not be remembered later if you ask the children what they did or said. On seeing the photograph, they instantly recall the moment and are able to talk about what they did. This cements the learning in their minds, and they can refer to it in future. If pictures are taken throughout the session, the children can stand back and comment on their learning. Prompts such as, 'What can you see happening here?' and 'Tell me about this' enhance the process. The pictures don't need to be printed; we sometimes use a digital projector to show the images. The children also love looking at the image on the LCD display on the back of the camera.

Using a video camera

Using a video camera can similarly enhance the development of self-assessment with children. They enjoy seeing what they did, and you can reinforce aspects of the learning as they watch. Most importantly, it is the *process* which is highlighted through this method, something which the children at this stage find difficult to understand and refer to. Debriefs are usually product-based, so this is a good way to get children to look at how they got there. They can celebrate all the stages along the way by viewing them on the video.

Feedback using puppets

As engaging as you may be as a teacher, children are often far more animated and responsive when a puppet is involved. We have a character called Hedley in our nursery, and he helps the children with their learning. At the end of a session, the children sit together to hear what Hedley saw. He provides feedback with comments such as, 'I saw Peter and Sam make a decision. I saw them shake hands' and 'I heard Millie ask if there was room for her to join in at the water tray'. By reinforcing the positive, these comments not only celebrate the achievements of our children, but also provide a gentle reminder to some of the others!

Feedback using photographs

These two children found it difficult to reach a decision. In the end, with the help of some adult intervention and mediation, one child backed down and agreed with the other in the name of making a decision. The children shook hands to symbolize the end of the process and to highlight the importance of decision making in the challenge. Capturing this moment with the camera served two purposes. For the children involved, it reinforced exactly what they did – and this will serve them well in future challenges. The photo also serves as a reminder to the other children that shaking hands is a valuable strategy in the process of making a decision.

Self-assessment

If children are to take responsibility for their own learning, then they need the tools to assess their work themselves. In this context, 'work' means their behaviour in classroom, their interactions with others and their skills – as well as the products they produce. For self-assessment to take place, then time needs to be allocated for reflection. We need to provide opportunities for children to reflect on their learning and on what they have achieved, as well as to acknowledge what is needed next time. When an opportunity occurs, it is our responsibility to make the most of it. Be ready with comments such as:

- 'What helped you solve the problem?'
- 'What did you need to do?'
- 'What happened?'

This will help the children begin to understand what they did and to be prepared for the next time they encounter a similar scenario.

Using stickers

When groups complete challenges, encourage them to review the product in a quick and simple way. You could have some printed stickers like this:

What I think
How I feel

Self-assessment stickers

The group can then discuss their responses and record them instantly on the sticker. This helps children to understand the importance of reviewing their work, gives them some vocabulary with which to assess it and, ultimately, helps to take the learning process on. The sticker is attached to the product and is displayed as an important element of the work for all to see. This shows parents and other visitors to the class that the children are capable of self-assessment and that it is valued as an assessment tool.

Using puppets

Tell the children that, for whatever reason (depending on the character of your puppet!) he or she has missed some of the session, and that it is their job to report back. Keep this general at first, to encourage all comments. As the children become familiar with this process, tailor it to the needs of the group by inviting comments on a specific area that relates to the skill being focused on. Provide the opportunity for your children to report back to the puppet in a private way, in order to build their confidence. When they are secure in this, offer them the opportunity to feed back and self-assess in a large group situation. This models the process for other children and highlights the value of it as a tool for learning.

ideas in action

A Eureka! moment

One day I was reminded how easy it can be to underestimate young children. A little girl was in the quiet room, deeply engaged in a conversation with Hedley. I asked her what they were chatting about. She replied, 'I'm telling Hedley about my train – he's been asleep.' This can only be described as a 'Eureka!' moment. I realized that Hedley could be used as a way of encouraging the children to reflect on their achievements through the day. I told them all that Hedley hadn't been able to see them working because he'd been dozing through the morning, and if they wanted they could tell him what he had missed. The comments came flying in: 'I let Sasha have a turn on the bike.' 'I did a peg pattern and it was all red.' The children were desperate to let Hedley know what he'd missed, and were unaware that they were entering into the valuable process of self-assessment.

Reviewing the session

In the key-worker group session at the end of the morning, you could include a simple 'Today at nursery I ...' activity. The children sit in a circle and take turns to tell the others what they have done. If this is done frequently, they usually become more confident and elaborate in their descriptions.

Peer-assessment

Encourage the children to comment on the work of others. One way to do this is to use 'Two stars and a wish', a strategy used by the King's College Assessment for Learning Team (Shirley Clarke, 2001). Start off by assessing the product, as the children find this easier than assessing the process. If a child has a painting or model, for example, ask the others to gather round to have a closer look. This immediately creates a community feeling, and promotes a culture of shared learning and shared success. The child with the product then chooses someone to comment on the work. This is important: it is their work and they should have control over who comments on it. Encourage comments that include detail, for example 'I like the wings because they've got glitter' or 'The eyes are big and they're shy'. These comments are the 'stars'. Then the children think about how they could help to improve the product – what could be done to make it even better. This becomes the 'wish'. Again, the child chooses someone to comment and the comment is accepted. It is usually framed in such a way that supports the learning process, for example 'Next time she could use glitter' or 'Next time there could be flowers too'. The children enjoy taking part in this process. The comments are recorded – for example on laminated cards (A5 size) and displayed in the class. Alongside the quotes from the children is the product itself – the painting or collage, for example – and a photograph of the children responding to the work, while the child holds it up for all to see. This strategy enhances the collaborative learning community and provides the children with the opportunity to take part in a peer-assessment process.

Peer-
assessment
templates

Using rubrics as an assessment tool

One of the most important aspects of the Critical Skills Programme is that the children set the standards for themselves. In other words, they decide what 'quality' should be, and aim to reach that when working though a challenge. If they fail to reach the standard they set, then they are in a strong position to identify what they did achieve and what they did not manage to achieve, because they decided on the levels from the outset.

The concept of a graded checklist of standards or levels of quality set by the children is known as a *rubric*, and can be used to raise standards in any classroom. The children decide the characteristics of a 'good' product, and identify the traits or attributes to be tracked. Each level of quality is outlined in terms of observables – things you can see or hear. The children should be able to identify each next step. Most children will be able to recognize their own performance level within the descriptors. For example, you could ask the children to decide what it means to have 'good waiting', and encourage them to choose three levels along a continuum. The use of photographs would be extremely helpful in this case, because the children can decide the specific observable behaviours to be displayed in each one, thus setting the quality criteria in the process. Having the continuum displayed in the class facilitates its use on an everyday basis, as necessary. The children can look at the photographs to identify where they think they are along the continuum as well as where they ought to be. The photographs provide all the information for the children to be able to meet the criteria.

Good sitting

We have used a trait continuum in our class to help the children with good sitting. By this we mean the following observables, as outlined by Nicola Call in *The Thinking Child*:

- ☆ bottom on the carpet
- ☆ facing the front
- ☆ hands in your lap
- ☆ looking at the speaker.

The children decided on photographs to show 'good sitting', 'nearly good sitting' and 'not really good sitting'. These are displayed in our classroom, and the children can refer to the images to see where they are and identify what they need to do to move themselves along the continuum.

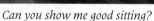

Can you show me good sitting?

Other possible subjects for a rubric include:

- ☆ Can you show me good listening?
- ☆ Can you show me good walking?
- ☆ Can you show me how to tidy up together?

Common problem

The biggest problem with feedback is that it is easy to let it slip. With so many observations and focused activities happening every day, it can be difficult to make time to actually debrief and feed back.

Possible solution

Make time! However you do it, feedback is the most important aspect of the teaching and learning process. We have an adult allocated to a 'follow-up' activity each day. This means that we can follow up the outcomes of our focused observations and let them have an impact on the learning almost instantly. In addition, we see the review or debrief as part of our routine, so whether it is done in a whole group, or in key-worker groups, we always make time for it. To neglect this aspect of teaching and learning is risk limiting children's success.

Key points

★ Consider, as a team, which aspects of self-assessment will work for you. If it's not practical and fairly quick, it'll never happen.

★ Try the drip-feed approach, allowing frequent opportunities for children to reflect.

★ Make the learning explicit; tell the children what they are doing and how it will help them in the future.

★ Be prepared for children who find it difficult to comment upon their work. Gently guide and support them. Use the other children to self-assess in front of the group, thereby modelling the process. As they gain experience, the more reticent ones will surprise you with their thoughts!

Chapter 7
Linking Critical Skills to early years practice

As early years practitioners, we are constantly observing our children in terms of the stepping stones and early learning goals laid out in the Curriculum Guidance document (2000). As teachers in a Critical Skills classroom, we observe and assess children against the critical skills and fundamental dispositions laid out in the CSP manuals. This chapter shows you how the two go hand-in-hand: by carrying out observations in the light of the critical skills you are also observing your children in relation to the early learning goals.

In this chapter, each critical skill and fundamental disposition is outlined and married with the relevant ELGs. This enables you to use the critical skills and fundamental dispositions in conjunction with the early learning goals to develop detailed assessments of your children. It means that incidental observations towards ELGs not only happen in a Critical Skills classroom, but can happen at the same time as assessment of skills and dispositions.

We will take each skill and disposition in turn, and look in detail at how it relates to the ELGs and to everyday early years classroom activity. For each critical skill or fundamental disposition, there is information under the following headings:

Links to ELGs

A list of early learning goals supported by this skill or disposition.

The skill or disposition in an everyday context

One of the fundamental principles of the Critical Skills model is that the skills are not developed through isolated challenges. In real life, problem-solving skills and creative thinking, for example, are called upon all the time – and this is the message to put across to the children. This section explains how, through the use of modelling, involving the children in explicit choices and reinforcing principles, these abilities can be developed in our children in the context of early years practice.

A child-speak script

In CSP, each critical skill and fundamental disposition has a script, which may be used by teachers, or coaches, to encourage its development. I have converted these into a child-speak format, appropriate for use with children at the foundation stage. This will be particularly helpful when working with members of staff (e.g. nursery officers and TAs) who may not have benefited from any formal Critical Skills training. The child-speak script can be used by them to coach the children. The scripts are also on the resources CD-ROM in a poster-style format that you may like to give to staff or to display on the classroom walls. They can then be referred to whenever the opportunity arises.

An example observation

In most early years settings, in accordance with the *Curriculum Guidance for the Foundation Stage*, children are regularly observed individually in a focused way. The real-life examples of observation provided here are intended to demonstrate what the skill or disposition looks like in action – and to encourage you to make your own observations in the context of the Critical Skills model.

★ PROBLEM SOLVING

Links to ELGs

Personal, social and emotional development

☆ respond to significant experiences, showing a range of feelings when appropriate;

☆ have a developing awareness of their own needs, views and feelings and be sensitive to the needs, views and feelings of others;

☆ form good relationships with adults and peers;

☆ work as part of a group or class, taking turns and sharing fairly, understanding that there needs to be agreed values and codes of behaviour for groups of people, including adults and children, to work together harmoniously;

☆ understand what is right, what is wrong and why;

☆ consider the consequences of their words and actions for themselves and others.

Communication, language and literacy

☆ interact with others, negotiating plans and taking turns in conversation;

☆ speak clearly and audibly with confidence and control and show awareness of the listener;

☆ use talk to organize, sequence and clarify thinking, ideas, feelings and events.

Mathematical development

☆ use developing mathematical ideas and methods to solve practical problems.

Problem solving in an everyday context

The 6-step mediation process developed by the High/Scope Educational Research Foundation can be a useful method for helping children to resolve disputes. Within this, the model for conflict resolution provides a strategy for children to solve their own problems, describing the stages that they must move through in order to reach a conclusion. It is the role of the teacher to explicate each stage along the way, therefore facilitating the process. Once established, this process can be used whenever conflict arises, with the level of teacher involvement decreasing each time, until the children are able to use the strategies to resolve conflicts among themselves:

1. Preparation, perspectives and strategies – have clear strategies in your mind before you approach the conflict
2. Acknowledge feelings – What is it? You look upset. What's the problem?
3. Gather information – What happened?
4. Restate the problem – So, let me get this right ... Is that what happened?
5. Ask for ideas for solutions and choose one together – Would it help if ...?
6. Be prepared to give follow-up support – offer to return in a little while to find out what they decided to do

Evans (2002)

At our nursery, we have developed this process through a regular feature known as 'the listening stop'. This is used whenever I feel there is a problem which all the children would benefit seeing worked through to a conclusion.

When such a problem arises, I call all the children together and we sit in a designated area with two comfortable chairs and a bus-stop-style sign. The two children involved in the conflict sit in the comfy chairs and we are ready to begin. I ask the children involved to say what the problem is, and then to explain to the others why this is a problem. Complaints such as, 'Well, Kai has the truck and I want to play with it' are the sort of thing usually aired. Once the problem has been verbalized, then all the other children can become involved. The next stage is to restate the issue for everyone involved, and agree that it is indeed a problem that needs solving. Then we ask the others to help – what could they do? Hear, perhaps, three or four suggestions, and encourage the children to use specific vocabulary, for example 'Would it help if ...?' The children involved then agree to go off together and choose one of the options. Having clapped to acknowledge a good meeting, all the children return to what they are doing. I then go back to the children involved after a couple of minutes and ask them what they have chosen. They explain how they have solved their problem and I ask the other children to congratulate them.

This process, as outlined in my book *Helping Young Children to Ask Questions* (2004), provides children with an effective strategy for becoming independent problem solvers.

Other ways to develop problem solving

☆ Texts can be used to support the development of the skill. Use a book as a starting point for discussion, asking children to choose their favourite page, and to say why they like it. (Cherrytree Books produce a series supporting the development of social skills and which is ideal for this type of activity.) The more you ask children their opinions about issues in books you share, the better they will be able to justify their preferences and verbalize their opinions. This type of language is a prerequisite if they are to solve problems for themselves.

☆ Use photographs to highlight problem-solving strategies. Show children talking to each other, shaking hands or asking others for help. Display these in a prominent place, perhaps alongside a listening stop, and refer to them whenever necessary.

☆ Take the opportunity when you debrief to tell children about problem solving that you have seen. This does not have to be at the end of a challenge; it could be part-way through or at the end of a session. Describe what you saw and what the children involved did. This provides children with more experience, and will help develop their ability to problem solve independently.

☆ Get a puppet to tell the children what he or she has seen. Sometimes when children are working, you can tune in to a particular group and hear vocabulary associated with problem solving. Comments such as, 'Now, I think that's a problem' are usually associated with a puzzled expression and a 'thinking noise' which sounds a bit like 'Hmmm'. When the puppet tells the children what he or she saw and heard, they are more likely to listen and take on board the strategies used.

☆ Look for problems and involve the class in solving them. Use everyday examples to show children that they are capable of solving problems. Try to use a consistent vocabulary and process – such as described by the High/Scope or listening stop models above. Always acknowledge the problem and explain why it is a problem. Issues to tackle could be, for example:

> Look at the blocks! There are so many on the carpet that Millie can't stand up there. She can't build anything because there are too many blocks. What could we do? I need your help.

Children, I've just noticed that it's raining and we need to go out and post our letter to Santa. If we go outside, we will get wet. What could we do?

The sign for nursery has come off the wall. We need to put it back so that visitors can find us. What could we do?

I've just noticed that there is water on the floor around the water tray. I don't want anyone to slip. I need your help. We could …

We need to go into the quiet room, but there are books on the floor. Some children have forgotten to put them back on the shelves and now there is a problem because we can't sit down in there. What could we do?

Child-speak script for developing problem solving

Child-speak script

- 🙂 You look angry/sad/upset. What is the problem?
- 🙂 Why is it a problem?
- 🙂 What do you need to do?
- 🙂 Would it help if …?
- 🙂 What could you use to help you?
- 🙂 Last time you did … Would that help you this time?
- 🙂 Go and try, and see if that works.
- 🙂 How do you feel now?
- 🙂 Shake hands: you've solved the problem.

Example of an observation illustrating problem solving

Stacey and Kai are playing in the small-world area. The jungle playmat is on the carpet, and there are five or six dinosaurs inside it.

'I'm looking for some dinner … roar!' says Kai, moving the dinosaur over the grass. Ryan kneels down, watching Kai and takes the dinosaur from Kai's hand. Kai responds, 'That one's mine, Ryan. No.'

Ryan states his intention: 'I want this one.'

Kai folds his arms, puts his head down and starts to cry.

Stacey, who has watched both boys, intervenes by approaching Kai.

'Are you alright, Kai?' Kai does not respond. Stacey looks at Ryan and says, 'Now there's a problem. Can you let Kai have a little go, and then you?' Ryan is aware, I suspect, of my hovering presence and agrees to take turns with Kai. I immediately move down onto the carpet and highlight the skill for the children.

'Stacey, you could see that Kai was upset and you wanted to help. You asked Ryan to share, and he said "yes". You solved the problem. Well done, Stacey. Ryan, you agreed to share – thank you. Remember next time to use words if you would like a turn. Kai, are you feeling better now?'

★ DECISION MAKING

Links to ELGs

Personal, social and emotional development

- ☆ respond to significant experiences, showing a range of feelings when appropriate;

- ☆ have a developing awareness of their own needs, views and feelings and be sensitive to the needs, views and feelings of others;

- ☆ form good relationships with adults and peers;

- ☆ work as part of a group or class, taking turns and sharing fairly, understanding that there needs to be agreed values and codes of behaviour for groups of people, including adults and children, to work together harmoniously;

- ☆ understand what is right, what is wrong and why;

- ☆ consider the consequences of their words and actions for themselves and others;

- ☆ select and use activities and resources independently.

Communication, language and literacy

- ☆ interact with others, negotiating plans and taking turns in conversation;

- ☆ sustain attentive listening, responding to what they have heard by relevant comments, questions or actions;

- ☆ speak clearly and audibly with confidence and control and show awareness of the listener;

- ☆ use talk to organize, sequence and clarify thinking, ideas, feelings and events.

Mathematical development

- ☆ use developing mathematical ideas and methods to solve practical problems.

Creative development

- ☆ respond in a variety of ways to what they see, hear, smell, touch and feel.

Decision making in an everyday context

As adults we make hundreds of decisions every day, many of which are subconscious. The need for decision making needs to be made explicit to children, as does the understanding that decisions are part of everyday life and help us to get on. We make a decision and act on it – and this affects what we do next. There are several ways not only to involve the children in a decision-making process, but to make them aware of what a decision is and why they need to make them all the time.

☆ Involve children in as many decisions as possible through the day, asking, for example:

> 'Which story would you prefer?'
>
> 'Shall we have the castle or the garage outside today?'
>
> 'Would you like water or milk with your snack?'
>
> 'Do you think we need more rockets on our display board?'

☆ Always look for a consensus, and make children aware that this is a method used for making a decision – for example, 'Seven children want this, but fourteen children have decided that they would prefer that.'

☆ Get children to show their decision by using their whole body. Ask them, for instance, to stand by the book that they would prefer to share. This makes the consensus clear and aids the decision-making process.

☆ Model the decision-making process for children, showing them that all the time you are making decisions that affect what happens in the classroom. When all the children are gathered together, ask the other adults present to help you make a decision – for example, 'I think it's too cold for a walk today, what do you think?' The children get used to this, and become keen to join in.

☆ Use the thumb tool. 'Would you rather cook biscuits or cakes?' A show of thumbs for biscuits gives the children a strategy they can use when they work independently.

☆ Use displays to raise the profile of decision making. Children can be involved in making pictograms and charts showing their preferences. You might, for example, use photographs of different areas of the classroom, and ask children to choose their favourite area. This will give you a good idea of the activities they enjoy, and helps you to plan accordingly. More importantly, you are showing children that you value their decisions.

☆ Use a carousel. The subject can be related to a book, a visit, planning a party or anything else you're doing. Questions related to books could include, for example:

> Do Bernard's parents not love Bernard, or are they just busy? (*Not Now Bernard* by David McKee)
>
> Do you think a Noo-Noo tree would grow in our garden? (*The Last Noo-Noo* by Jill Murphy)
>
> Do trees really grow in Max's bedroom, or is it just a dream? (*Where the Wild Things Are* by Maurice Sendak)
>
> Was it a good idea to build all those things where the flowers used to grow? (*Dinosaurs and All That Rubbish* by Michael Foreman)
>
> Should the teachers have stopped Michael from making a rocket? (*Michael* by Tony Ross)

These questions may seem advanced, but the more discussion time you spend in groups, the more advanced children's thinking skills become, and the more they are able to articulate their thoughts and decisions.

☆ Wherever possible, give children a choice. This makes the process of making a decision easier, because they will be more used to choosing. And if you offer only two options each time, it will be easier for children to see the implications of each choice and so to make an informed decision.

Child-speak script

Child-speak script for developing decision making

🙂 Why do we need to decide? (seeing the need for a decision)

🙂 What might happen if you choose ...? (entering into the decision-making process)

🙂 You need to choose. (reaching a decision)

🙂 Do you think this is a good idea? (looking at options, seeking advice)

🙂 Why don't you see what (child's name) thinks? (seeking opinions)

🙂 Why have you chosen/decided that? (being equipped either to compromise or to defend an opinion)

🙂 This is what you have decided. (taking responsibility for actions)

🙂 How do you feel? What do you think? (reaching a decision)

Example of an observation illustrating decision making

Laura, Megan and Lohren are sitting in the quiet room. Freya is standing in the book corner and is pretending to be the teacher.

'Now you need to choose.' She picks up three books from the display and puts them on the carpet. She directs the other three girls.

'Stand by the book you want.' The girls get up and move to a book, all three choosing the same story. Freya continues, 'Okay I'll read this one.' And she takes the book and sits on the sofa. The other children sit on the rug and listen as Freya reads to them. At this point I intervene:

'What a good idea, girls. Sometimes we have to choose and standing by our favourite is something we do sometimes, isn't it? You helped to make a decision, Freya. Well done!'

The children have clearly re-created a scenario that the whole group had previously experienced with me, but this has provided them with a decision-making tool that they were able to apply independently.

⭐ CRITICAL THINKING

Links to ELGs

Personal, social and emotional development

- ☆ continue to be interested, excited and motivated to learn;
- ☆ be confident to try new activities, initiate ideas and speak in a familiar group;
- ☆ understand what is right, what is wrong and why;
- ☆ consider the consequences of their words and actions for themselves and others.

Communication, language and literacy

- ☆ interact with others, negotiating plans and taking turns in conversation;
- ☆ sustain attentive listening, responding to what they have heard by relevant comments, questions or actions;
- ☆ speak clearly and audibly with confidence and control and show awareness of the listener;
- ☆ use talk to organize, sequence and clarify thinking, ideas, feelings and events.

Mathematical development

- ☆ use developing mathematical ideas and methods to solve practical problems.

Knowledge and understanding of the world

- ☆ investigate objects and materials by using all of their senses as appropriate;
- ☆ find out about, and identify, some features of living things, objects and events they observe;
- ☆ look closely at similarities, differences, patterns and change;
- ☆ ask questions about why things happen and why things work;
- ☆ observe, find out about and identify features in the place they live and in the natural world;
- ☆ find out about their environment, and talk about those features they like and dislike.

Physical development

- ☆ recognize the importance of keeping healthy and those things which contribute to this;
- ☆ recognize the changes that happen to their bodies when they are active.

Creative development

- ☆ respond in a variety of ways to what they see, hear, smell, touch and feel;

☆ express and communicate their ideas, thoughts and feelings by using a widening range of materials, suitable tools, imaginative and role play, movement, designing and making, and a variety of songs and musical instruments.

Critical thinking in an everyday context

As teachers we habitually use critical thinking. Every time we carry out an activity, we consider questions such as: What are the implications? Why did the children find this particular activity difficult? Every day we have to be open minded, to judge the credibility of sources, to deduce and induce, and to be well informed. Similarly, the skill of critical thinking has to be modelled so that children do it without really being aware of it.

☆ When helping children to resolve conflicts, stress the importance of gathering the facts, hearing opinions and only then making a decision based on all the information.

☆ Show children that you are open minded. Always give opportunity for them to share their ideas and, where possible, exhaust these before stepping in. Prompts such as 'Any other ideas?' demonstrate the importance you place on their input.

☆ Display questions around the room to prompt critical thinking:

> What do you think?
>
> Does anybody else have anything to share?
>
> Why do you think that happened?
>
> Do you agree?

☆ Refer to critical thinking in the debrief, raising the profile of the skill and reinforcing the process for children. Make thinking explicit, for example:

> 'We could have used paper, but because we know it goes soggy in water, we decided to use plastic instead.'
>
> 'We knew that biscuits would not take long to cook, so we decided to make those today.'
>
> 'We listened to everyone's ideas for the colour, and decided that Sarah's idea to paint the animal green was a good one because it would be hidden in the trees.'
>
> 'Peter thought that Ryan looked upset, and we could tell because he was crying.'

Child-speak script for developing critical thinking

Child-speak script

☺ What do you think about that idea? (encouraging a response to a proposal)

☺ What is good about the idea?

☺ What don't you like about the idea?

☺ Why do you think this happened? (seeking a cause)

☺ Do you think that might work? Why? Why not? (finding a workable solution)

☺ How else could we get help? (pooling different sources to seek an answer)

☺ Is there anything else we could do? (exploring all options)

☺ Do you think this might work better than that? (encouraging comparison)

☺ What have we done about this? (acting on a situation)

Example of an observation illustrating critical thinking

Luc and Philip are outside playing on the soft surface with a Brio train set. They are joining pieces of track together, getting more pieces out from the box and adding them on in turn. They take turns in conversation and listen to one another.

'Put that one on the end, Philip.'

'Okay,' says Philip.

The boys add on a piece of track that goes up to form a kind of flyover, then find the connecting piece which brings the track down to ground level again. However, every time they let go of the track, it breaks and falls to the floor. Luc has an idea.

'Hold it there, Philip.'

For a few seconds, Philip holds the bridge in place with his hands and Luc carries on connecting the other pieces of track. Then Philip has an idea.

'I'll get a block.' Luc carries on, but Philip goes into the block area. He collects a small solid block and runs back outside. Luc watches as Philip puts the block underneath the bridge part of the track.

The block holds the track in place and the boys carry on building. I take a photo of their track to show the other children later, then intervene.

'Philip, what was the problem?' I let him explain what he did and then continue. 'You knew that the block was strong and that it would stay still underneath your bridge. Even though the block wasn't here, you went and collected it to make it work. What good thinking, Philip. Well done!'

★ CREATIVE THINKING

Links to ELGs

Personal, social and emotional development

☆ continue to be interested, excited and motivated to learn;

☆ be confident to try new activities, initiate ideas and speak in a familiar group;

☆ respond to significant experiences, showing a range of feelings when appropriate;

☆ select and use activities and resources independently.

Communication, language and literacy

☆ interact with others, negotiating plans and taking turns in conversation;

☆ sustain attentive listening, responding to what they have heard by relevant comments, questions or actions;

☆ extend their vocabulary, exploring the meanings and sounds of new words;

☆ speak clearly and audibly with confidence and control and show awareness of the listener;

☆ use talk to organize, sequence and clarify thinking, ideas, feelings and events.

Mathematical development

☆ use developing mathematical ideas and methods to solve practical problems.

Knowledge and understanding of the world

☆ investigate objects and materials by using all of their senses as appropriate;

☆ find out about, and identify, some features of living things, objects and events they observe;

☆ ask questions about why things happen and why things work;

☆ build and construct with a wide range of objects, selecting appropriate resources, and adapting their work where necessary. Select the tools and techniques they need to shape, assemble and join materials they are using;

☆ observe, find out about and identify features in the place they live and in the natural world;

☆ find out about their environment, and talk about those features they like and dislike;

☆ physical development;

☆ move with confidence, imagination and safety;

☆ travel around, under, over and through balancing and climbing equipment.

Creative development

☆ explore colour, texture, shape, form and space in two or three dimensions;

☆ use their imagination in art and design, music, dance, and imaginative and role-play stories;

☆ respond in a variety of ways to what they see, hear, smell, touch and feel;

☆ express and communicate their ideas, thoughts and feelings by using a widening range of materials, suitable tools, imaginative and role play, movement, designing and making, and a variety of songs and musical instruments;

Creative thinking in an everyday context

It is our responsibility, as early years practitioners, to develop the capacity of our children to think creatively, and to give them the confidence to do so. If we create a culture of trust and security in the classroom, children will feel relaxed and safe enough to take creative risks. This is a vital, lifelong skill that children need to acquire if they are to become confident and successful learners.

☆ Celebrate success. When a problem has been solved creatively, photograph it, tell everyone about it and show children that there is no problem that they cannot solve.

☆ Involve children in planning activities. Christmas party planning is a good one; the children can decide which games they would like to play and what food they would like to eat. These experiences give children the opportunity to share their ideas in a safe environment where they know their thoughts will be valued and considered.

☆ Involve children in changing a role-play area. They can make lists of what will be needed, and help to think of imaginative alternatives using the resources available. They can help to rearrange the furniture, verbalizing their creative thinking as they work alongside others.

☆ Give children the opportunity to feed off each other's ideas, perhaps recording these in the form of a mind map. This way, you can model the writing process, record their thinking and highlight how ideas link together to form a bigger, collective idea.

Child-speak script for developing creative thinking

Child-speak script

🙂 Can we solve the problem in another way? What else could we do? (seeking new solutions)

🙂 Why do you think that?

🙂 Do you think it would be helpful to …? (considering other viewpoints)

😊 Let's put all our ideas together on our board (brainstorming solutions)

😊 Is there a problem with that idea? (sifting out unworkable suggestions)

😊 Does anyone have any other ideas? (encouraging any thoughts, even if they seem unrelated)

😊 What would … think about this? (different perspectives)

Example of an observation illustrating creative thinking

Jake is in the block area with Oliver, Keiran and Kai. He is holding a wooden truck and watching the other three boys. Kai looks at Jake.

'Only airport trucks are allowed,' he says. Jake smiles, clearly thinking about this, as he watches Oliver and Kieran playing with the planes on the 'runway'. He replies by asking Kai a question.

'Can you take me to Manchester?'

'OK, jump in my airport truck and I'll take you,' says Kai.

The children play in an imaginative way and show signs of responding to changing ideas through their interaction and conversation. As this observation develops, Kai and Jake become more involved in the travel aspect of the conversation and begin talking about where they had been on holiday. (Jake has family living in Manchester, hence the original question.)

★ COMMUNICATION

Links to ELGs

Personal, social and emotional development

☆ continue to be interested, excited and motivated to learn;

☆ be confident to try new activities, initiate ideas and speak in a familiar group;

☆ respond to significant experiences, showing a range of feelings when appropriate;

☆ have a developing awareness of their own needs, views and feelings and be sensitive to the needs, views and feelings of others;

☆ form good relationships with adults and peers;

☆ work as part of a group or class, taking turns and sharing fairly, understanding that there needs to be agreed values and codes of behaviour for groups of people, including adults and children, to work together harmoniously;

☆ understand what is right and wrong and why;

☆ consider the consequences of their words and actions for themselves and others;

☆ understand that people have different needs, views, cultures and beliefs, that need to be treated with respect.

Communication, language and literacy

- ☆ interact with others, negotiating plans and taking turns in conversation;

- ☆ enjoy listening to and using spoken and written language, and readily turn it into their play and learning;

- ☆ sustain attentive listening, responding to what they have heard by relevant comments, questions or actions;

- ☆ extend their vocabulary, exploring the meanings and sounds of new words;

- ☆ speak clearly and audibly with confidence and control and show awareness of the listener;

- ☆ use talk to organize, sequence and clarify thinking, ideas, feelings and events.

Mathematical development

- ☆ in practical activities and discussion begin to use the vocabulary involved in adding and subtracting;

- ☆ use everyday words to describe position;

- ☆ use developing mathematical ideas and methods to solve practical problems.

Knowledge and understanding of the world

- ☆ investigate objects and materials by using all of their senses as appropriate;

- ☆ find out about, and identify, some features of living things, objects and events they observe;

- ☆ ask questions about why things happen and why things work;

- ☆ find out about part and present events in their own lives, and in those of their families and other people they know;

- ☆ find out about their environment, and talk about those features they like and dislike.

Physical development

- ☆ move with confidence, imagination and safety;

- ☆ show awareness of space, of themselves and of others.

Creative development

- ☆ explore colour, texture, shape, form and space in two or three dimensions;

- ☆ use their imagination in art and design; music, dance, and imaginative and role-play stories;

- ☆ respond in a variety of ways to what they see, hear, smell, touch and feel;

- ☆ express and communicate their ideas, thoughts and feelings by using a widening range of materials, suitable tools, imaginative and role play, movement, designing and making, and a variety of songs and musical instruments.

Communication in an everyday context

As early years practitioners, we understand the importance of speaking skills because they facilitate so much of what children do. Without good speaking skills, they can struggle to share ideas and experiences, their ability to take turns is restricted and they can find asking questions or seeking clarification very difficult. These impact heavily on the day-to-day running of the classroom. Children without good speaking skills can lack confidence, display frustration and become involved in regular conflicts. Research shows that an indicator of a child's reading age at ten years is their vocabulary at the age of three (EPPE). As teachers, we seek to develop independent and inquisitive learners, who can resolve conflicts themselves, take risks and defend a point of view. In order to maximize learning, it is our duty to develop good speaking and listening skills with our children. There are several ways to develop communication skills in the classroom:

☆ Establish a quality audience. This might be in terms of good listening – as outlined by Nicola Call in her book *The Thinking Child*. Once children understand what it means to be a good listener, they have specific observable behaviours to work towards. These become a prerequisite whenever somebody is speaking, whether an adult or a child, and become an underlying expectation which facilitate the communication process.

☆ Use photographic rubrics to show good sitting or good listening. This makes it easy to refer children to them, should they need reminding.

☆ Give the children plenty of opportunity to talk to one another. Let them turn to the person next to them to talk about a particular subject, and encourage turn taking around the circle.

☆ Encourage children to speak in front of the whole group. We bought a children's microphone and were amazed to find that even our most reserved children wanted to come out and give everyone a rendition of their favourite song!

☆ Provide real telephones. We have an internal phone system and two phones at opposite ends of the nursery that children can use. The number to dial is displayed alongside the phone, and those buttons are shaded. Ensure that the facility to get an outside line or contact the emergency services is disabled!

☆ Model the use of the telephone as a skilful way to communicate. When taking the register, for example, phone the secretary to see if she knows why a particular child has not arrived. Children will then see the advantage of communicating in this way.

☆ Encourage children to ask questions over the telephone. Ring the headteacher to see if he or she can come and hear some singing, or ask the secretary if she would like some toast for a snack. Find real reasons for communicating, developing children's ability to listen and pass on information.

☆ Encourage children to communicate by asking questions on your behalf or by passing on information. 'Can you ask Mrs Morin if she would like a glass of water, please?' or 'Please could you ask Mrs Walker to bring the camera when she comes outside?'

☆ Model communication through letter writing. Write thank you letters after visits, read out responses and raise the profile of writing as a means of communication.

☆ Provide communication boxes for each child and plenty of paper and pencils. The children will enjoy writing notes to each other and placing them in each other's communication box. Label each one and have a photograph alongside the name, to assist recognition. Empty them regularly – our children check their boxes on their way home every day.

☆ Provide opportunities for children to express their feelings. Resources such as the 'box of feelings' are great for this. Look at photographs and drawings, asking children to say what they feel about them, and why. Play games where children have to show different facial expressions, for example: a sad face, a happy face or a scared face. All these activities reinforce the importance of feelings and facilitate children's ability to share their feelings with you.

☆ The resource book *Helping Young Children to Speak With Confidence* (Bayley and Broadbent, 2003) has further suggestions for activities to develop communication skills. These include a chimpanzee called Kofi as the tool for emotionally engaging the children.

Child-speak scripts for developing communication

Child-speak script

☺ Can we let the others know what we think?

☺ Tell the others what we have decided. (summarizing)

☺ What do you think about this? What do you think this means? (interpretation)

☺ Can you say that another way? (verifying meaning)

☺ Can you show me good listening?

☺ How can you tell if someone has good listening?

☺ Let's get together and see how things are going. (keeping communication going when at a distance)

☺ Do you know what (child's name) is saying? Do you understand?

☺ Don't start until everyone's eyes are looking at you? Have your audience got good listening?

Example of an observation illustrating communication

Observation of children in the age-old 'show and tell' can provide a good deal of insight into their communication development. When the children come together in the morning, I often ask them if they have any news, something to share or something to show us. Here is a simple observation of a child who was willing to communicate with the group.

Millie puts her hand up and says, 'I've done a picture.' I ask her if she would like to show the others and she agrees by nodding with a smile. Millie stands next to me, facing the other children, who are sitting cross-legged on the carpet. She turns away from me to face them, holds her painting in front of her so that all the children can see, and says, 'I did this at home with my mummy. There's a tree and that's Bella, my doggie.' When she has finished, I ask the children if they would like to say or ask anything, and a couple of hands go up. Millie chooses Phoebe, who asks, 'Is that in your garden?' to which Millie replies, 'Yes'. In order to highlight the skills associated with communication to both Millie and the rest of the group, I speak to them directly.

'Do you know, I'm so proud of Millie because she came and told everyone about her work. She looked at you all and she spoke really clearly so that everyone could hear what she had to say. Could you all see her painting? (children nod) That's because she held it up. What a good idea! Thank you, Millie. You were thinking about your audience and what they needed. You (directed at the group) were such a good audience. I was watching you and you were sitting still, with your hands in your laps and you were all looking at Millie so that she knew you were listening. Phoebe asked a question, and Millie listened to her and then gave her answer. Thank you.' At this point the children give Millie and themselves a clap, and Millie returns to the carpet.

★ ORGANIZATION

Links to ELGs

Personal, social and emotional development

☆ continue to be interested, excited and motivated to learn;

☆ be confident to try new activities, initiate ideas and speak in a familiar group;

☆ have a developing awareness of their own needs, views and feelings and be sensitive to the needs, views and feelings of others;

☆ work as part of a group or class, taking turns and sharing fairly, understanding that there needs to be agreed values and codes of behaviour for groups of people, including adults and children, to work together harmoniously;

☆ dress and undress independently and manage their own personal hygiene;

☆ select and use activities and resources independently.

Communication, language and literacy

☆ interact with others, negotiating plans and taking turns in conversation;

☆ sustain attentive listening, responding to what they have heard by relevant comments, questions or actions;

☆ extend their vocabulary, exploring the meanings and sounds of new words;

☆ speak clearly and audibly with confidence and control and show awareness of the listener;

☆ use talk to organize, sequence and clarify thinking, ideas, feelings and events.

Mathematical development

☆ Use developing mathematical ideas and methods to solve practical problems.

Knowledge and understanding of the world

☆ find out about, and identify, some features of living things, objects and events they observe;

☆ ask questions about why things happen and why things work.

Physical development

☆ move with confidence, imagination and safety;

☆ move with control and co-ordination;

☆ show awareness of space, of themselves and of others.

Creative development

☆ express and communicate their ideas, thoughts and feelings by using a widening range of materials, suitable tools, imaginative and role play, movement, designing and making, and a variety of songs and musical instruments.

Organization in an everyday context

The important thing here is to lead by example. We cannot expect our children to look after their things, plan their day and be able to revise their plans if we have piles of papers lying around and can't find the key for the outdoor shed! Organization links strongly to routine, and there are several ways to develop this skill:

☆ Model the organization of time. Explain that if three other children help to tidy the block area, you will all be finished more quickly.

☆ Model the organization of materials. Provide clear storage containers to encourage independence, or stick on photographs of what is inside. Have regular clear outs, so that the drawer labelled 'shells' actually does contain shells. Involve children in this where possible, encouraging them to take responsibility and ownership for their learning environment, and to appreciate the advantages of being organized.

☆ Involve children in the organization of tasks. Make a daily To Do list – sometimes with the children – and explain who will carry out what, when and with whom. This should be a work-in-progress list, so it is important that you refer back to it. Part-way through the session, call all the children together, ask them to tick off what has been achieved, add on anything else that is needed, and rub off anything that has changed. It is important that children see the value of this kind of list and that it is flexible, not set in stone. Refer back to the list at the end of the session as a way of feeding back, recalling and debriefing, and celebrating achievement. This is sometimes a good time to compile the To Do list for the following session.

☆ Model prioritizing by explaining why a particular job has to be done first, for example, 'Shopping is the first job, because otherwise we won't have any fresh fruit for our snack. Once we've had our snack, we can begin our collage work.' This helps the children to understand that not all jobs can be done at once, and that some jobs are more important than others.

☆ Use choosing boards to help children organize their play. We have three boards (one for each key-worker group) and they each display a number of photographs showing the areas of the nursery available to the group. These include photos of the role-play area, the construction area, the small-world area, the maths table, the graphics area, the computers, and so on. The children know that each photograph represents the area rather than the particular activity that is depicted in the photo. Children find their labelled pegs and attach them to the area they would like to visit. If a particular child needs refocusing, we direct them back to their choosing board to decide on an activity they would like to do. This helps the children to organize themselves, and provides them with the opportunity for variety. As teachers, we monitor the areas they are choosing and may suggest alternatives, according to their individual needs.

☆ Establishing a routine is crucial to the development of organization as a skill. Our children register themselves when they enter nursery. In this way, we all know who is absent and the children view this process as an important part of what they do at nursery. When they go home, they take off their Velcro name and photograph and replace it on their key-worker board.

☆ Allocate roles as a way of modelling organization. Give each key-worker group an area of the nursery to tidy up, which avoids duplication of effort or something being left out. Alternatively, create a 'jobs board'. Our board depicts a number of jobs, which could be anything from picking up Duplo to sweeping the sand to watering the plants. There are enough jobs for one for every child, and there is also a photo of each child. Children look at the board to find their photo and see what their role is for the day. The jobs can be swapped around as often as you see fit, but model organization at a high level.

Child-speak script for developing organization.

Child-speak
script

- 😊 Could we do this in a better way? (encouraging efficiency)
- 😊 What do you think we should do first? Why? (prioritizing)
- 😊 What will happen if we don't get this part finished? (prioritizing)
- 😊 Could we do this in a quicker way? (achieving goal within time constraints)
- 😊 What do we want? (goals)
- 😊 What will we do next time? Will we …? Why not? (avoiding repeating inefficiency)
- 😊 What could we use to help us? (appropriate tools)
- 😊 Can we get this done in time for our snack? (introducing time frames)
- 😊 Has everybody got a job to do? (responsibility)

Example of an observation illustrating organization

Jack is in the block area with Macy, and together they are building a harbour. In preparation for their building work, they have tipped out lots of blocks onto the carpet – to the point where there is not much carpet space left in the area. William enters the block-play area. He looks at the children building and at their harbour, and he looks at the floor. He is standing on a large block and as he moves, his foot slips off the block and onto the carpet. He picks up a large block to replace it on the shelf. He is careful not to choose part of the harbour. Jack notices what William is doing and calls over.

'William, we're not tidying up.'

'We might trip,' replies William, who puts the block away. Jack continues playing with Macy, and William replaces two or three of the blocks before I approach to ask them what they are doing. While Macy and Jack carry on playing, William answers, 'It's a mess and it's a problem.'

I ask the other two to listen, and I praise William by restating the action.

'William, when you came in here you nearly fell, didn't you? You could see that it was difficult to build with so many blocks already on the carpet. What did you decide to do?'

'Put them away,' he replies.

'In nursery, we sometimes need to be tidy and put things away as we go along. It helps us to keep organized, doesn't it? Thank you, William, for being organized.'

⭐ MANAGEMENT

Links to ELGs

Personal, social and emotional development

- ☆ continue to be interested, excited and motivated to learn;

- ☆ be confident to try new activities, initiate ideas and speak in a familiar group;

- ☆ have a developing awareness of their own needs, views and feelings and be sensitive to the needs, views and feelings of others;

- ☆ form good relationships with adults and peers;

- ☆ work as part of a group or class, taking turns and sharing fairly, understanding that there needs to be agreed values and codes of behaviour for groups of people, including adults and children, to work together harmoniously;

- ☆ dress and undress independently and manage their own personal hygiene;

- ☆ select and use activities and resources independently.

Communication, language and literacy

- ☆ interact with others, negotiating plans and taking turns in conversation;

- ☆ sustain attentive listening, responding to what they have heard by relevant comments, questions or actions;

- ☆ extend their vocabulary, exploring the meanings and sounds of new words;

- ☆ speak clearly and audibly with confidence and control and show awareness of the listener;

- ☆ use talk to organize, sequence and clarify thinking, ideas, feelings and events.

Mathematical development

- ☆ use developing mathematical ideas and methods to solve practical problems.

Knowledge and understanding of the world

- ☆ find out about, and identify, some features of living things, objects and events they observe;

- ☆ ask questions about why things happen and why things work.

Physical development

- ☆ move with confidence, imagination and safety;

- ☆ move with control and co-ordination;

- ☆ show awareness of space, of themselves and of others.

Creative development

☆ express and communicate their ideas, thoughts and feelings by using a widening range of materials, suitable tools, imaginative and role play, movement, designing and making, and a variety of songs and musical instruments.

Management in an everyday context

By seeing management modelled, children come to understand that tasks need to be assigned fairly, that they need to support each other in their work, and that regular check-ups on progress keep everyone on task. Management is a fairly tricky set of skills to develop, but it is possible.

☆ When allocating tasks, help children by using visual images. For example, a cake case together with a photo of all the children who will be involved in the cake-baking activity, could be stuck onto the list of things to do. This is a good way to model task-assignment, and will help children to allocate tasks and roles when they work in groups on challenges.

☆ Offer tasks and roles: 'Who would like to help by offering to …' Take every opportunity to thank the children, letting them know that they are a valuable part of the team.

☆ Have regular check-ups to see how things are going, perhaps with each group sharing with the others what they have done.

☆ Use all the skills the children have experienced and developed through problem solving, decision making and creative thinking to negotiate solutions to problems. Involve them, value their thoughts and make it clear that the solution has come from them.

Child-speak script for developing management

Child-speak script

😊 (Child's name), what is your job?

😊 Does everyone have a job to do? (assigning roles fairly)

😊 Tell me what you are going to do? What do you need to do? (restating the task for clarification)

😊 What are the things that we need to get done? What do we need to do?

😊 Can you help each other out?

😊 If there is a problem, how might you work it out? What could you do?

😊 Who would be the best person to do this job? Why do you think that? (applying individual skills)

😊 What things do we always do well? (considering collective talents)

Example of an observation illustrating management

Management is a difficult skill to observe because it involves children helping others to optimize their work, and sometimes these moments are hard to catch. In our nursery, the children have a choosing board where they can go and attach a named peg to a photographic representation of a learning area in the classroom. This helps the children to plan their session. It is also a tool that helps us to refocus off-task children, and an aid in the feedback and review session. The children quite often hear one of us redirect someone back to their choosing board if they are distracted or wandering, and are used to hearing advice such as, 'I think it would help if you went back to your choosing board and had another think.' The children also know that running in nursery is not safe and are used to hearing comments such as, 'I'm glad that you're playing so well together, girls, but next time can you remember to walk in nursery?' This modelling is such a big part of nursery life; as we manage the children, we are providing them with the skills to manage themselves and one another.

Roseanna is sitting on the carpet with some construction materials, a hammer and some bolts. She looks up and sees Megan run across the carpet and fall down onto her knees. Roseanna watches as Megan gets up and starts turning herself around in circles.

'Megan, I think you need to go back to your choosing board!' says Roseanna (in a tone, embarrassingly enough, not too dissimilar to mine). Megan can see that I am sitting nearby, and she looks at me.

'What do you think, Megan? What have you chosen?' I ask her.

Megan looks around for an area to choose.

'Roseanna had a good idea. If you go back to your choosing board, you could have another look at everything together, and choose again. What do you think?'

Megan nodded and went back to the board. I sat next to Roseanna.

'Why did you help Megan?' I asked her, to which she replied, 'She was running.'

I brought our conversation to a close.

'I could see that you were busy, and you noticed that Megan wasn't. You knew that the choosing board would help her to get busy again. What a good friend, Roseanna.'

★ LEADERSHIP

Links to ELGs

Personal, social and emotional development

- ☆ continue to be interested, excited and motivated to learn;
- ☆ be confident to try new activities, initiate ideas and speak in a familiar group;
- ☆ have a developing awareness of their own needs, views and feelings and be sensitive to the needs, views and feelings of others;
- ☆ form good relationships with adults and peers;

☆ work as part of a group or class, taking turns and sharing fairly, understanding that there needs to be agreed values and codes of behaviour for groups of people, including adults and children, to work together harmoniously;

☆ dress and undress independently and manage their own personal hygiene;

☆ select and use activities and resources independently.

Communication, language and literacy

☆ interact with others, negotiating plans and taking turns in conversation;

☆ sustain attentive listening, responding to what they have heard by relevant comments, questions or actions;

☆ extend their vocabulary, exploring the meanings and sounds of new words;

☆ speak clearly and audibly with confidence and control and show awareness of the listener;

☆ use talk to organize, sequence and clarify thinking, ideas, feelings and events.

Mathematical development

☆ use developing mathematical ideas and methods to solve practical problems.

Knowledge and understanding of the world

☆ find out about, and identify, some features of living things, objects and events they observe;

☆ ask questions about why things happen and why things work.

Physical development

☆ move with confidence, imagination and safety;

☆ move with control and co-ordination;

☆ show awareness of space, of themselves and of others.

Creative development

☆ express and communicate their ideas, thoughts and feelings by using a widening range of materials, suitable tools, imaginative and role play, movement, designing and making, and a variety of songs and musical instruments.

Leadership in an everyday context

Some children are natural leaders. They assume control when things start to go wrong, they recognize when something needs to be changed and they are confident to challenge others. Other children need to be shown how to lead. They need to be coached, encouraged and praised so that they can begin to see themselves as leaders, and to see the advantages of taking on this role, for themselves and for others.

☆ Promote individual responsibility. When all the children are gathered together, ask for a volunteer to wipe the board, sweep the leaves or deliver a letter to another class. Give the responsibility out publicly, and let the children involved know that it is now their responsibility to carry out the task. Always thank the children in advance for their co-operation and involvement, and reinforce this during feedback time when the task has been carried out (hopefully with success!).

☆ Articulate your vision to the children to ensure that expectations are clear: explain, for example, that the twigs need to be collected into black sacks; that books need to be replaced so that they match the photograph; that we always walk in the classroom.

☆ Capitalize on every opportunity. If a child approaches you with a problem, let him or her be the one who articulates the situation to the others. The child can take suggestions and choose a suitable solution. This gives individual children the opportunity to assume the role of leader.

☆ Model clear values, and ensure that these are shared. If it has been agreed that the children will look after the things in the classroom, then ensure that they understand the need for this agreement and the consequences if it is not adhered to. Always lead by example: so if children understand that 'we walk in nursery' to avoid accidents and to keep them safe, don't run across the room (unless it is a safety issue).

Child-speak script

Child-speak scripts to develop leadership

☺ What do we need to do first? (taking the lead, prioritizing)

☺ How are we going to do it? (direction)

☺ Have you listened to everyone? (responsibility and initiative)

☺ Does everyone know what they are doing? (guiding vision)

☺ Can you check that no one needs your help? (ensuring that individuals fulfil commitments)

☺ What will you do if there is a problem? (handling conflict)

☺ Maybe an adult might be able to help you out. (seeking higher ground)

☺ I think (child's name) needs a job. Can you think of a job for them to do? (encouraging involvement)

Example of an observation illustrating leadership

Timothy is playing by himself in the block area. He is clearly constructing with a purpose in mind, using both hands to move blocks and create a tunnel for the cars to go through. He catches my eye and has a big smile on his face. Yasmine and Laura enter the block area.

'Can we play?' Laura asks.

'Yes you can,' replies Timothy.

At this point I am concerned, because Timothy clearly has an idea of what he wants to build and has been enjoying working by himself. But he passes a block to Yasmine.

'Put that there and then the cars go under it,' he says.

All three begin to play together, taking ideas, roles and responsibilities from Timothy.

The two girls know that Timothy had a plan and know it is a good one. They are happy to be led by a leader. Timothy knows that the other children can help and is willing to delegate roles that will ultimately enhance the outcome.

On this occasion I didn't feel it appropriate to engage with the children, as they were progressing so well on their own. I did, however, make a note of these personality traits and abilities, which could enhance future work.

⭐ OWNERSHIP

Links to ELGs

Personal, social and emotional development

- ☆ continue to be interested, excited and motivated to learn;
- ☆ be confident to try new activities, initiate ideas and speak in a familiar group;
- ☆ have a developing awareness of their own needs, views and feelings and be sensitive to the needs, views and feelings of others;
- ☆ form relationships with adults and peers;
- ☆ work as part of a group or class, taking turns and sharing fairly, understanding that there needs to be agreed values and codes of behaviour for groups of people, including adults and children, to work together harmoniously;
- ☆ consider the consequences of their words and actions for themselves and others;
- ☆ select and use activities and resources independently.

Communication, language and literacy

- ☆ interact with others, negotiating plans and taking turns in conversation;
- ☆ sustain attentive listening, responding to what they have heard by relevant comments, questions or actions;
- ☆ extend their vocabulary, exploring the meanings and sounds of new words;
- ☆ speak clearly and audibly with confidence and control and show awareness of the listener;
- ☆ use talk to organize, sequence and clarify thinking, ideas, feelings and events.

Mathematical development

☆ use developing mathematical ideas and methods to solve practical problems.

Knowledge and understanding of the world

☆ investigate objects and materials by using all of their senses as appropriate;

☆ find out about, and identify, some features of living things, objects and events they observe;

☆ look closely at similarities, differences, patterns and change;

☆ ask questions about why things happen and why things work;

☆ observe, find out about and identify features in the place they live and in the natural world;

☆ find out about their environment, and talk about those features they like and dislike.

Physical development

☆ move with confidence, imagination and safety;

☆ show awareness of space, of themselves and of others.

Creative development

☆ express and communicate their ideas, thoughts and feelings by using a widening range of materials, suitable tools, imaginative and role play, movement, designing and making, and a variety of songs and musical instruments.

Ownership in an everyday context

Ownership goes hand in hand with responsibility. We want our children to believe in their own capabilities, to feel empowered to take action, to engage in decision making at various levels and to see the importance of taking risks.

☆ Provide children with opportunities to believe in their own capabilities. One of the most powerful ways of doing this is by celebrating their successes. At this stage, there are several milestone achievements which are cause for celebration. In our nursery, we have a 'We can do it' board, where we share successes. These include being able to put on socks and shoes independently, being able to zip up a coat, being willing to try something new for snack. When a child has one of these moments, we take a photograph and add it to the success board. Parents enjoy sharing the good news, and it is a powerful way of raising the profile of ownership. At the same time, it helps to develop the classroom community and a shared culture of celebrating success.

☆ Encourage children to take responsibility for their outcomes, for example: 'The animal is green, because that's the colour you decided would be best' or 'We haven't added stars to our tree because we decided we didn't need them.'

☆ Encourage honesty as children begin to take responsibility for their own actions. When resolving conflict, ensure that any child involved apologizes, if that is the action they consider necessary.

☆ Provide opportunities for children to work collaboratively, and observe them as they do so. You are then in a position to help them to celebrate their joint achievement. Encourage each child to verbalize what their individual contribution has been, and how it fits within the whole. Use questions such as, 'What did you do?' and 'How do you feel?' to promote ownership.

☆ Praise children who take control. Feeding back and commenting on remarks such as 'We need a garage to go with the house' and 'Shall we build a station too?' helps to raise the profile of ownership and develops the children's concept of ownership as a desirable attribute.

Child-speak scripts for developing ownership

Child-speak
script

☺ What do you think?

☺ If you were doing this without your friends to help you, how would you do it?

☺ Who would be the best person to do this? (skills)

☺ Whose job is it to finish the …? (responsibility)

☺ What do you think about how things are going so far?

☺ Are you proud of the people working with you, and of what you're doing together?

☺ You want to change … Why do you want to do that? Why do you think that is a good idea?

☺ Could it go wrong if you change it? Have you thought about what might happen if you …?

☺ Which part did you do? How did you help? (individual contributions)

☺ Good idea! How will you do it?

☺ Is this the best that it can be? (satisfaction)

☺ Can we make up our minds? Do we need to see what the others think? (making decisions)

Example of an observation illustrating ownership

When children bring in a book to share, they often put it on the edge of the whiteboard. Usually, at some point during the day we will get the chance to share it together.

Phoebe brings in a French book, showing common foods and their names in French. I intend to look at this with the children quite briefly and then send the book home. However as I begin showing the children, they start repeating the words for cheese, bread and so on, and are keen to carry on. Later in the morning, they choose the book over another popular story and we have another 'French lesson'. I don't really think that much more about it, other than to notice that their level of interest had surprised me.

Next morning, however, two other children bring in French books from home, and this is followed by another book and a set of flashcards the next day. Parents have started asking if we have been learning French, because Marley had asked for 'fromage' in his sandwiches and William had asked his mum at bath time if he could have a 'glace'! Taking learning outside school is a key feature of ownership, so these children were certainly taking responsibility for their own learning. We decided to capitalize on this by having a French week with songs, numbers, a French café role play and crêpes. We invited parents in for a French coffee morning, complete with croissants, *pains au chocolat* – and Edith Piaf! The children planned the whole event and followed it through, taking ownership of the week throughout.

★ SELF-DIRECTION

Links to ELGs

Personal, social and emotional development

   ☆ continue to be interested, excited and motivated to learn;

   ☆ be confident to try new activities, initiate ideas and speak in a familiar group;

   ☆ have a developing awareness of their own needs, views and feelings and be sensitive to the needs, views and feelings of others;

   ☆ form relationships with adults and peers;

   ☆ work as part of a group or class, taking turns and sharing fairly, understanding that there needs to be agreed values and codes of behaviour for groups of people, including adults and children, to work together harmoniously;

   ☆ consider the consequences of their words and actions for themselves and others;

   ☆ select and use activities and resources independently.

Communication, language and literacy

   ☆ interact with others, negotiating plans and taking turns in conversation;

   ☆ sustain attentive listening, responding to what they have heard by relevant comments, questions or actions;

   ☆ speak clearly and audibly with confidence and control and show awareness of the listener;

   ☆ use talk to organize, sequence and clarify thinking, ideas, feelings and events.

Mathematical development

   ☆ use developing mathematical ideas and methods to solve practical problems.

Knowledge and understanding of the world

☆ investigate objects and materials by using all of their senses as appropriate;

☆ find out about, and identify, some features of living things, objects and events they observe;

☆ look closely at similarities, differences, patterns and change;

☆ ask questions about why things happen and why things work;

☆ build and construct with a wide range of objects, selecting appropriate resources, and adapting their work where necessary. Select the tools and techniques they need to shape, assemble and join materials they are using;

☆ observe, find out about and identify features in the place they live and in the natural world;

☆ find out about their environment, and talk about those features they like and dislike.

Physical development

☆ move with confidence, imagination and safety;

☆ show awareness of space, of themselves and of others.

Creative development

☆ express and communicate their ideas, thoughts and feelings by using a widening range of materials, suitable tools, imaginative and role play, movement, designing and making, and a variety of songs and musical instruments.

Self-direction in an everyday context

Self-directed children display high levels of motivation, persistence, independence and confidence. They are inquisitive, they question, and they seek solutions. To develop self-direction, it is the responsibility of the teacher to provide opportunities for children to take.

☆ Provide activities which prompt questions. For instance, wet sand in the sand tray with water wheels could elicit questions about why the sand cannot pass through – and a desire to find out why. Other examples might include:

floating and sinking materials in the water tray

a collections of magnets and objects on the science table

a collection of boxes, tubes and piping outside

a train track to set up with one piece missing.

☆ Help children to value advice by first making the offer and then letting them make the decision about whether to accept. 'Can I help?' or 'Would you like my help?' gives them the option. Learning to take advice is an important component of self-direction.

☆ Being independent is another part of self-direction. It can be tempting, when teaching in the early years, to help children more than they really need. Asking, 'Do you think you need my help?' encourages them to work together without your intervention. Praise them if they are able to do it, reinforcing their teamwork, independence and confidence.

☆ Encourage reflection as a crucial aspect of self-direction. If children are to move their learning forward, they need to assess what they have done, evaluate it and decide on a course of action for next time. Try to evaluate with the children as frequently as you can, so that it becomes part of the classroom routine. Ask them what they enjoyed about the work, and encourage them to suggest what they could do to improve it next time. With experience, their responses will shift from product-based assessment to a deeper level of process-based reflection.

Child-speak script

Child-speak scripts for developing self-direction

☺ If you were doing this without your friends to help you, how would you do it?

☺ Is there anything you need to know before you start? (gathering information)

☺ How can you find that out? Who could you ask to help you?

☺ Where do we go if we want to find out something new?

☺ Do you need to know this before you start?

☺ Can any of your friends help you?

☺ How are you going to find this out? (pursuing enquiry)

☺ What do you need to know? What would you like to find out? (goals and clarification)

☺ If that doesn't work, where else might you look? (further support)

☺ Show me where you found this. Tell us how you know this. (sources)

Example of an observation illustrating self-direction

Francisco is sat at a table with a group of other children. The independent activity there is cutting and sticking, and there are piles of birthday cards, sheets of paper, glue sticks and scissors (ready for the children to develop their own learning experiences).

'I need the glue,' Francisco says. He looks around, picks up a glue stick and sticks his pictures onto his sheet of paper. He picks up another card and begins to cut around the shape. He stays at this activity until his piece of paper is full. He turns to the child sitting next to him.

'Look at this; it's beautiful isn't it?' he says. Not really interested in a reply, he continues, 'I'm going to do my name. I can do it.' He then puts his work in the red box, ready to go home, and chooses something else. I approach Francisco at this point.

'Francisco, what careful work! How do you feel?'

'Good.' Francisco is beginning to articulate his own success here, just as he did when he turned to another child for affirmation.

'You should feel very proud. Think of all the things you had to do – fetch the glue, cut out the shapes, stick them in a space, and write your name. You should feel good. Well done!'

⭐ QUALITY

Links to ELGs

Personal, social and emotional development

- ☆ continue to be interested, excited and motivated to learn;
- ☆ be confident to try new activities, initiate ideas and speak in a familiar group;
- ☆ have a developing awareness of their own needs, views and feelings and be sensitive to the needs, views and feelings of others;
- ☆ form relationships with adults and peers;
- ☆ work as part of a group or class, taking turns and sharing fairly, understanding that there needs to be agreed values and codes of behaviour for groups of people, including adults and children, to work together harmoniously;
- ☆ understand what is right, what is wrong and why;
- ☆ consider the consequences of their words and actions for themselves and others;
- ☆ select and use activities and resources independently.

Communication, language and literacy

- ☆ use talk to organize, sequence and clarify thinking, ideas, feelings and events.

Mathematical development

- ☆ use developing mathematical ideas and methods to solve practical problems.

Knowledge and understanding of the world

- ☆ investigate objects and materials by using all of their senses as appropriate;
- ☆ find out about, and identify, some features of living things, objects and events they observe;
- ☆ look closely at similarities, differences, patterns and change;
- ☆ ask questions about why things happen and why things work;
- ☆ observe, find out about and identify features in the place they live and in the natural world;

☆ find out about their environment, and talk about those features they like and dislike.

Creative development

☆ express and communicate their ideas, thoughts and feelings by using a widening range of materials, suitable tools, imaginative and role play, movement, designing and making, and a variety of songs and musical instruments.

Quality in an everyday context

Quality, in terms of standards in the early years, can be described in child-speak terms as 'as good as it can be'. We want our children to strive for the best, and to stop only when they are convinced that what they have done is 'the best that it can be', and that their effort is 'the most that it could be'.

☆ Set the standard. Make it explicit that the standard you expect from the children is the highest it can possibly be. Then they will come to expect it of themselves and will begin to take responsibility for setting their own standards.

☆ Model striving for improvement. Ask the children: 'Are you happy with this?' 'Could we make it better?' 'Is there anything else we need to add?' 'Do you think this is good enough?' 'What do you think?' This will filter down into other independent activities that they carry out.

☆ Let children set their own standards and decide what quality is. 'What do you think I'd like to see when you are playing at the water tray this morning?' (Children with aprons on, sharing, taking turns, etc.) Children cannot meet expectations if they don't know what they are. You must make them explicit if you want quality from them. Let them decide on the photographs to show good sitting. Then they will be able to set their own, achievable and measurable standard – one that is not out of reach because they have set it themselves.

☆ Include quality as part of your Full Value Contract. Our contract includes the phrase 'We try our best', which is accompanied by a photograph of a child displaying a high level of concentration at the writing table. Refer back to this to remind the children that this is one of the things they have agreed to. When reviewing and reflecting, ask them whether or not they think they have tried their best, and encourage justification either way.

Child-speak scripts for developing quality

Child-speak script

😊 Are you happy with this work? Tell me what you think.

😊 Is this as good as it can be? Tell us about it.

😊 Is this what we wanted it to be like? Do you think it is the same? (referring to quality criteria, which may be as simple as a sketch)

😊 If you were to make it even better next time, what could you do? How could you make it better? (changing criteria)

☺ How did we know what we wanted it to look/be like? (setting criteria at the start)

☺ How can you tell that everybody is ready to listen? Why is it important that we wait? (quality audience)

☺ So that everyone can hear you, what do you need to think about before you start? What might happen otherwise? (quality presentation)

Example of an observation illustrating quality

The 'Two stars and a wish' device (see page 71) relates to quality, because the children not only try their best, but establish quality criteria themselves. Rather than respond to a piece of work by saying 'I like the sky', comments such as, 'I like the sky because it's at the top and it's blue' show quality criteria beginning to develop.

★ CHARACTER

Links to ELGs

Personal, social and emotional development

☆ be confident to try new activities, initiate ideas and speak in a familiar group;

☆ have a developing awareness of their own needs, views and feelings and be sensitive to the needs, views and feelings of others;

☆ have a developing respect for their own cultures and beliefs and those of other people;

☆ form relationships with adults and peers;

☆ work as part of a group or class, taking turns and sharing fairly, understanding that there needs to be agreed values and codes of behaviour for groups of people, including adults and children, to work together harmoniously;

☆ consider the consequences of their words and actions for themselves and others;

☆ understand that people have different needs, views, cultures and beliefs, that need to be treated with respect;

☆ understand that they can expect others to treat their needs, views, cultures and beliefs with respect.

Communication, language and literacy

☆ interact with others, negotiating plans and taking turns in conversation;

☆ sustain attentive listening, responding to what they have heard by relevant comments, questions or actions;

☆ speak clearly and audibly with confidence and control and show awareness of the listener.

Knowledge and understanding of the world

☆ look closely at similarities, differences, patterns and change;

☆ find out about past and present events in their own lives, and in those of their families and other people they know;

☆ observe, find out about and identify features in the place they live and in the natural world;

☆ find out about their environment, and talk about those features they like and dislike;

☆ begin to know about their own cultures and beliefs and those of other people.

Physical development

☆ move with confidence, imagination and safety;

☆ show awareness of space, of themselves and of others.

Creative development

☆ express and communicate their ideas, thoughts and feelings by using a widening range of materials, suitable tools, imaginative and role play, movement, designing and making, and a variety of songs and musical instruments.

Character in an everyday context

One of the ELGs for personal and social development details an understanding of what is right and wrong, but the development of character as a fundamental disposition goes beyond this. We want our children to have convictions, integrity, respect for others and themselves, construct judgements and have principles.

☆ Take every opportunity to help children to show compassion towards others and to try and help. If a child is upset, ask the others what they could do to help.

☆ Promote the use of kind hands/feet/words, in an attempt to develop a culture of mutual respect.

☆ Use published material to prompt discussion and raise awareness of 'the right thing to do'. Stories such as *It's My Turn* and *Bad Mood Bear* are good for this, as is the Cherrytree series, which promotes social skills such as friendship, taking turns and sharing. These are particularly helpful because they show children of similar age encountering issues that are common in an early years setting.

☆ A puppet is a useful tool here. Develop a character who can be a bit of a rebel – not sharing toys, taking snack without saying 'thank you', or throwing things on the floor. When discussing an issue with children, ask the question 'What would you do?', and give them the opportunity to share their views and offer their thoughts and suggestions in a safe environment.

☆ Show children that you trust them. Once in a while, give them the chance to shine. 'Usually we would line up group by group, but I think I can trust you to line up quietly at the same time. I know I won't see any pushing and all that I will hear will be gentle voices. I know I can trust you.' Children love rising to challenges like these, and provide you with a great opportunity to heap praise upon them!

Child-speak scripts to develop character

Child-speak script

☺ Why have you decided to do that? (questioning assumptions or values; driving decisions)

☺ Do the others know how you feel? (encouraging awareness of feelings/opinions)

☺ If you do …, then … might happen. Is this OK with everyone? (understanding consequences)

☺ This is what you did. What do you think about that? Was that the right thing to do? Why do you think that? (ethics)

☺ Do you think you did the right thing?

☺ Will this make everybody happy?

☺ What do you really think? What is important to you? (principles)

☺ What is your job? (responsibilities)

Example of an observation illustrating character

In nursery, we are always looking for children who act honestly and in a right way, and who are sensitive to the needs of others. When these occasions arise, we give praise because the children need to know that these things do not go unnoticed; that they are appreciated and are desirable features of their personalities.

Macy is playing in the water tray. The water is green and there are small jewels at the bottom (which the children call 'treasure') and some sieves. Macy has collected all the jewels and put them into one sieve. She is holding this with two hands when Emily comes over and puts an apron on.

'Can you put them back in the water, Macy?' asks Emily.

Macy looks at the jewels.

'OK,' she replies. She tips the jewels back into the water tray, and Emily starts collecting them in one of the sieves. I am just about to approach the children when Emily responds.

'Thank you. We can share them now, can't we?'

Later on in the session when all the children are together, I ask Macy and Emily to come to the front and I explain what happened.

'Wasn't that a kind thing to do? Macy knew that Emily wanted to share the jewels and she let her. What a good friend.'

★ COLLABORATION

Links to ELGs

Personal, social and emotional development

- ☆ respond to significant experiences, showing a range of feelings when appropriate;

- ☆ have a developing awareness of their own needs, views and feelings and be sensitive to the needs, views and feelings of others;

- ☆ form good relationships with adults and peers;

- ☆ work as part of a group or class, taking turns and sharing fairly, understanding that there needs to be agreed values and codes of behaviour for groups of people, including adults and children, to work together harmoniously;

- ☆ understand what is right, what is wrong and why;

- ☆ consider the consequences of their words and actions for themselves and others.

Communication, language and literacy

- ☆ interact with others, negotiating plans and taking turns in conversation;

- ☆ speak clearly and audibly with confidence and control and show awareness of the listener;

- ☆ use talk to organize, sequence and clarify thinking, ideas, feelings and events.

Mathematical development

- ☆ use developing mathematical ideas and methods to solve practical problems.

Collaboration in an everyday setting

One of the ultimate aims for a Critical Skills classroom is that children see the advantages of working together. Collaboration goes beyond co-operation, and involves contribution, engagement, agreement, a shared vision and a notion of 'buying in'.

- ☆ Provide opportunities for children to work collaboratively:

    Work with children in the block-play area to construct together.

    Provide shared resources, for example, Duplo, which facilitate collaboration.

    Remove chairs around the small-world table to encourage free flow and an overlapping of play.

    Provide large floor puzzles rather than smaller, table-top ones – encouraging children to work together.

Aid the process of collaboration by having two water wheels but only one jug, therefore prompting collaboration (sometimes via a squabble!).

Cover the easel with one large sheet rather than small, individual sheets. Then children can contribute to a shared piece of work. Celebrate this during the debrief and value it by displaying it somewhere prominent.

Similarly, cover the writing table with newsprint from a roll, encouraging collaboration, often through a process of co-operation first.

☆ Praise those children who collaborate, and highlight this to the other children. 'Daniel decided that there was too much for him to do by himself, so he went to find a helper. He asked Kieran if he would like to help, and Kieran said "yes". They worked together – and look at their rocket now! Well done for working together, boys. I think we should give them a clap.'

☆ Model the importance of collaboration as a way of optimizing work. 'Nursery needs tidying up and I need your help. We need to work together so that we have time to go for a walk before lunch. Can you help me? Can we all work together?' Children love rising to the challenge, so ensure it is achievable. At the end of the task, make sure you reinforce the advantages of collaboration as well as celebrating their success. 'I couldn't have done all this without your help. Well done, team! We worked really well together'.

Child-speak scripts to develop collaboration.

Child-speak script

😊 Show me your thinking faces. Let's get all our ideas together.

😊 Can you think of a good way to help you decide? (making decisions)

😊 Have you asked if anyone knows the answer?

😊 What is a good way of making sure everyone has a turn?

😊 If somebody didn't want to join in, what could you do to help?

😊 What could we do better in our group next time?

😊 Who is good at doing what in this group? Who enjoys painting/writing/drawing? (using skills)

😊 Did everyone know what they had to do? (getting clarity within the group)

😊 What did you decide at the beginning? (identifying goals)

😊 How could you work even better in your group? Would you change anything for next time? (setting future goals)

😊 Did you listen to what everyone had to say? (getting contributions)

😊 Did everyone have a job to do? (assigning roles)

😊 Can everybody do something?

☺ Does everyone feel proud of this? ('buying in')

☺ Is everyone pleased with what you have done in your group? (group support)

Example of an observation illustrating collaboration

Being able to work as part of a group is almost a prerequisite for a successful day in nursery; in any case, it certainly facilitates it. The children work in a group during challenges, but this is very focused, and collaboration is emphasized at other times. By observing children during free-flow play, it is possible not only to identify, praise and highlight collaboration, but to gain an insight into group dynamics as they progress to challenges.

Freya is sitting at the maths table. She has a pegboard in front of her, and is making a pattern with the pegs. She has made one row of yellow pegs and one row of blue pegs. She is making her third line – another row of yellow. Ryan comes up to the table and watches Freya for a few seconds.

'Shall I get one for you?' he says. He looks into the tray of pegs and picks out two yellow pegs, handing these to Freya.

'Thanks,' says Freya, as she takes them and adds them to her pattern.

'Do you want to help?' she asks.

Ryan sits on the chair next to her and holds the tray, while Freya continues the pattern.

'I need a blue one,' says Freya, and Ryan searches through the tray. The children stay here for several minutes.

A simple 'You're working together' is enough acknowledgement in this situation.

★ CURIOSITY AND WONDER

Links to ELGs

Personal, social and emotional development

☆ continue to be interested, excited and motivated to learn;

☆ be confident to try new activities, initiate ideas and speak in a familiar group;

☆ understand what is right, what is wrong and why;

☆ consider the consequences of their words and actions for themselves and others;

Communication, language and literacy

☆ interact with others, negotiating plans and taking turns in conversation;

☆ sustain attentive listening, responding to what they have heard by relevant comments, questions or actions;

☆ speak clearly and audibly with confidence and control and show awareness of the listener;

☆ use talk to organize, sequence and clarify thinking, ideas, feelings and events.

Mathematical development

☆ Use developing mathematical ideas and methods to solve practical problems.

Knowledge and understanding of the world

☆ investigate objects and materials by using all of their senses as appropriate;

☆ find out about, and identify, some features of living things, objects and events they observe;

☆ look closely at similarities, differences, patterns and change;

☆ ask questions about why things happen and why things work;

☆ observe, find out about and identify features in the place they live and in the natural world;

☆ find out about their environment, and talk about those features they like and dislike.

Physical development

☆ recognize the importance of keeping healthy and those things which contribute to this;

☆ recognize the changes that happen to their bodies when they are active.

Creative development

☆ explore colour, texture, shape, form and space in two or three dimensions;

☆ use their imagination in art and design, music, dance, imaginative and role play and stories;

☆ respond in a variety of ways to what they see, hear, smell, touch and feel;

☆ express and communicate their ideas, thoughts and feelings by using a widening range of materials, suitable tools, imaginative and role play, movement, designing and making, and a variety of songs and musical instruments.

Curiosity and wonder in an everyday context

To me, this is what early years education is all about. The most successful learners ask questions, show a sense of curiosity, and enquire. They have a love of discovery – and it is our responsibility, as educators, to foster this quality; to nourish it, embrace it and enhance it in our children. Then they will have every chance of becoming lifelong learners.

☆ Provide children with opportunities to ask questions. To do this, they need to know what a question is, to know how to form one, and to see the value of questioning as a tool for enhancing understanding. *Helping Young Children to Ask Questions* (Charlesworth, 2004) offers some ways to do this through case study.

☆ Spend as much time as you can outside. Go for walks, run on the school playing fields, jump in puddles in the rain. Do whatever it takes to get your children enquiring about the world around them. Let them stand and look at worms, admire spider webs and blow bubbles with soapy water. The world really is a wondrous place, and as adults we can take this for granted. Try to see these marvels through the eyes of a three or four year old.

☆ Take risks and do things differently. If you usually walk a certain way, then walk along another route. If you usually have snack indoors, then have it outdoors once in a while. As important as routine is, so is change.

☆ Follow the interests of the children. One day our children watched the school caretaker cleaning our windows. They were fascinated as the soapy water obscured their view and the scraper made everything crystal clear again. Make the most of these moments. We nipped out at lunchtime and bought buckets, sponges and scrapers. The children spent all afternoon cleaning the windows again (much to the caretaker's outward dismay, but secret delight!). This is what curiosity and wonder is all about.

☆ Provide for 'what if' moments.' Ask children questions before you cut open a melon, or before you introduce a new puppet. Build suspense and get their imaginations going into overdrive. With independent activities, provide investigative materials: mirrors outside, magnifying glasses and binoculars for walks, metal detectors for the sand pit or squidgy things in feely boxes. Keep them on their toes and keep them guessing.

☆ Tell them a story without using a book, letting them imagine the scene in their heads. Describe a magical world while they lie down on the carpet with their eyes closed. Play some atmospheric music to enhance this.

Child-speak scripts to develop curiosity and wonder

Child-speak script

☺ Could we do this another way?

☺ How else could you let us know about this? (demonstrating understanding)

☺ What is the best part about this? (interest)

☺ What would you like to find out? (learning)

☺ If you wanted to know something, who could help you? (pursuing learning)

☺ How could we do this better?

- Even if it doesn't work, could you try something else?
- What would happen if …?
- What else could you do to get there?
- How would you go about …? Just say what you think.
- What would be the best way to …?

Example of an observation illustrating curiosity and wonder

We want our children to question the world around them, and it is our responsibility, as teachers, to equip them with the skills to enable them to do this. The notion of a question, what it is, how it is formulated and how it can help further their learning all need to be made explicit to children. We do this using a puppet (Hedley), and get the children to the stage where they ask him what they would like to find out. However, Hedley cannot answer all their questions.

'Mrs Charlesworth, what happens to the boats?'

I look at Jake and try to help him out. Does he mean the boats at nursery which were in the water tray the previous day, or the boats in the harbour which are ready for scrapping? I ask him to clarify this,

'I'm not sure what you mean, Jake. Which boats?'

'The boats, what happens to the boats?' he repeats. I try a different approach.

'When?'

'When they go in the triangle.'

It takes a minute for the penny to drop. He is asking me about the Bermuda Triangle! It transpires that Jake has seen a television programme about the subject. Hedley can answer *some* questions, but we need to 'Ask Jeeves' as well for this one.

Having equipped the children with an understanding of a question and having modelled how questions can help them, we observe the children displaying the confidence to question the world around them.

★ COMMUNITY

Links to ELGs

Personal, social and emotional development

- ☆ respond to significant experiences, showing a range of feelings when appropriate;
- ☆ have a developing awareness of their own needs, views and feelings and be sensitive to the needs, views and feelings of others;
- ☆ have a developing respect for their own cultures and beliefs and those of other people;
- ☆ form good relationships with adults and peers;

☆ work as part of a group or class, taking turns and sharing fairly, understanding that there needs to be agreed values and codes of behaviour for groups of people, including adults and children, to work together harmoniously;

☆ understand what is right, what is wrong and why;

☆ consider the consequences of their words and actions for themselves and others;

☆ understand that people have different needs, views, cultures and beliefs, that need to be treated with respect;

☆ understand that they can expect others to treat their needs, views, cultures and beliefs with respect.

Communication, language and literacy

☆ interact with others, negotiating plans and taking turns in conversation;

☆ sustain attentive listening, responding to what they have heard by relevant comments, questions or actions;

☆ speak clearly and audibly with confidence and control, and show awareness of the listener;

☆ use talk to organize, sequence and clarify thinking, ideas, feelings and events.

Knowledge and understanding of the world

☆ find out about past and present events in their own lives, and in those of their families and other people they know;

☆ observe, find out about and identify features in the place they live and in the natural world;

☆ find out about their environment, and talk about those features they like and dislike;

☆ begin to know about their own cultures and beliefs and those of other people.

Community in an everyday context

This is one of the most important of all skills and dispositions to develop because it is prerequisite for all the others. Children need to feel safe, secure, valued, respected and understood if they are to take risks, make decisions, solve problems or collaborate.

☆ Ensure that children feel valued as part of the group. Use words such as 'we', 'team' and 'us' when referring to them. Whenever there is a problem, refer to it as a collective problem: something that is everyone's responsibility and that they will need to work on together in order to solve. The problem may be a very small thing (water spilling out of the water tray, for example) but the aim is the same: to get children to take a collective responsibility for their learning environment.

☆ Develop a Full Value Contract, because this involves everyone and binds everyone together by its shared values and expectations.

☆ Produce work together, work in a whole group and model the concept of helping others to achieve a common goal.

If you are in any doubt about the strength of your classroom community, then return to Chapter 2 which details more ways to develop this.

Child-speak scripts to develop community

Child-speak script

☺ How do we know what to do in our class? (rules, expectations, FVC)

☺ We all like different things, don't we? We're not all the same, are we? (diversity)

☺ How do we keep each other safe?

☺ How do we look after each other? (mutual respect)

☺ How do we help each other? (affecting one another's learning)

☺ (using video material) What can you see happening? (observing interaction of the group)

☺ Could you say that in another way? (seeking acceptance)

☺ What does your group think of that idea?

☺ How can we be kind to one another? (respect)

☺ You solved a problem What will you do next time? (conflict resolution)

☺ Did everyone try their best? Did everyone have a go? Did everyone do their job?

Example of an observation illustrating community

Contributing to the maintenance of the nursery is part of a developing sense of community.

Phoebe is in the home corner with two other children and Mrs Walker, a nursery officer. She takes a netted skirt off and attempts to hang it up. After a couple of failed attempts with the skirt falling off the hanger, she passes the skirt to Mrs Walker.

'Can you do this, please?'

'Shall I help you Phoebe? These are tricky, aren't they? Well done for trying. It's important to keep things tidy in here, so hanging the skirt up is a good idea.'

Mrs Walker notices that Stacey doesn't have her shoes on, as she has been dressing up too. She asks her to replace them if she has finished dressing up, and tells her that someone might stand on her toes.

'You might cry,' says Phoebe. Phoebe uses her existing knowledge to help Stacey to understand why she needs her shoes on, thus showing a sense of community. Phoebe then helps Lohren to lay the table. She takes cups out of the dishwasher and hands them to Lohren.

'You need this,' she says.

Mrs Walker praises Phoebe for helping Stacey and Lohren, and for wanting to hang the skirt up. 'You want everyone to have a good time in nursery and you're so helpful Phoebe. Thank you.'

Common problem

Having a time for 'Critical Skills' is not the way forward with this approach and will cause you problems.

Possible solution

The Critical Skills approach needs to be adopted in its entirety and has to be in the back of your mind all the time you are working with children. It is important to take every opportunity to raise awareness of the skills, to consolidate them and to deepen understanding. Having Tuesday as the day that you 'do a challenge', will mean that you miss out on all the problem solving, leadership, organization and decision making that goes on under your nose the rest of the time! Once you know what you're looking for, you'll find it everywhere.

Key points

★ Try to familiarize yourself with the eight critical skills and seven fundamental dispositions. Use the poster on the CD and put it up somewhere you'll see it. It won't be long before you remember them.

★ Don't try and do too much at once. Focus on one skill or disposition, familiarize yourself with it and work on it with the children. Once you are familiar with where the links are to the ELGs, it is far easier to bring Critical Skills in alongside what you are already doing. It is not something new – it helps you to do what you are already doing.

★ Spend time with your nursery officers helping them to familiarize themselves with the approach. Although this may take time, it will be time well spent – the more pairs of eyes observing, the better!

Chapter 8
Progressive indicators of achievement

When we are observing children against the critical skills and fundamental dispositions, it can be difficult to gauge to what extent the skill or disposition is being displayed. In other words, two children might display elements of an understanding of decision making, but one might have a deeper understanding than the other. The progressive descriptors below will help you to pinpoint what stage individual children have reached in the development of each critical skill (rather than simply recording that that skill has been observed) and to identify the next learning step in the development of that skill. They are intended to be used one at a time, as each skill is targeted. The descriptors could be used as an aide-memoire as you coach during a challenge, or as a point of discussion with all staff members at the end of a challenge. Either way, the process will give you a detailed picture of overall development within the class, and will help you decide whether more modelling is required.

Whether the children reach level three in the first year of the foundation stage depends partly on the children themselves – all children are different, and all groups are different. It will also depend on the level at which you model these skills and on the opportunities you provide for the children to develop them. In the case of our nursery class, the number of children achieving level three rose in the second year of working within this model. It could probably be expected that, in an early years classroom where the Critical Skills model has been established, the majority of the class would be working between levels two and three by the end of the foundation stage.

However, it is important not to get hung up on the descriptors. They are simply a tool to help identify where the children are in order to help them to advance their learning. They are certainly not intended as a checklist of achievement to be recorded as 'evidence' or kept in a file for the next teacher.

Progressive indicators of critical skills

The table below shows each critical skill as described in the Critical Skills Programme alongside three stages in the development of that skill at foundation stage level.

These can be used as you work with children to help you to observe and assess a particular skill. You could take the three stages and consider each child according to what you already know, and in the light of what you observe during the challenge.

Skill	1	2	3
Problem solving 'Capable of developing effective solutions to the multidimensional and complex problems ever present in personal and professional arenas'	• Can acknowledge a problem and think of a solution with adult intervention	• Can independently suggest solutions and can resolve the issue with some support	• Can find an effective solution, communicate this and resolve the issue independently
Decision making 'Are capable decision makers who can and do make responsible decisions in diverse situations'	• Can listen to options and accept a choice	• Can listen to options and make own choice	• Can decide from a range of options, justify the choice and understand the need for a decision
Critical thinking 'Can routinely and effectively apply critical thinking in a range of life roles'	• Can listen to the thoughts and ideas of others as they apply their thinking to a range of practical situations	• Can be heard to question others • Is beginning to offer own ideas and reflect on the ideas of others	• Can think laterally, apply existing knowledge to new problems, and seek reasons
Creative thinking 'Have the confidence in and capacity for the creative thinking that both enhances experience and results in a variety of life roles'	• Can use play to re-create real-life situations which build on recent experiences	• Can demonstrate creative ideas, which challenge convention, and can carry these out with support • Can create imaginary roles in play	• Can play imaginatively and in a fluid way, responding to the changing ideas of others • Has the confidence to try something new and think 'outside the box'
Communication 'Are skilful communicators who express themselves with clarity and authenticity'	• Can speak to close friends about personal experience	• Can speak to a small group of children in a clear way and can respond to questions with support	• Can speak with confidence to the whole group, in a clear voice and giving eye contact, understanding the needs of the audience
Organization 'Can efficiently and productively organize time, space, materials and tasks'	• Can put some resources away, usually with reassurance • Knows that there are key features to the structure of the day	• Can put things away when reminded; understands that the main features of the day come in an order (e.g. lunchtime and then home time)	• Can understand that it is helpful to keep things tidy and is able to help other children to put things away properly • Can structure the day in terms of routine • Can use a learning environment independently and creatively

Skill	1	2	3
Management 'Can skilfully help others to optimize their work together through effective management'	• Can choose a favourite activity and sustain interest for a short period of time • Can see an activity to its conclusion with encouragement	• Can usually choose and carry out tasks independently for a short period of time, and will refocus when reminded	• Can choose and carry out tasks independently over a sustained period of time • May offer reminders to children who appear off task
Leadership 'Can recognize quality leadership and can assume it when appropriate'	• Can parallel play • Follows the example of a friend	• Can share suggestions and ideas with others if given encouragement • Shows signs of leadership in play activities, valuing the qualities of others	• Can share ideas with others enthusiastically, offering suggestions and workable solutions • Can develop play scenarios and delegate roles to others

Progressive indicators of fundamental dispositions

These can be used as you work with children to help you to observe and assess a particular disposition. You could take the three stages and consider each child according to what you already know, and in the light of what you observe during the challenge.

Disposition	1	2	3
Ownership 'Responsible and invested owners of lifelong learning'	• Can find aspects of learning interesting when they have direct links to personal experiences • Can talk about own point of view with encouragement	• Can find some aspects of own learning interesting, showing signs of ownership • Takes responsibility when prompted • Starts to enter into decision-making processes	• Can take responsibility for own learning and behaviour, asking questions and actively seeking answers • Takes learning outside school setting
Self-direction 'Reflectively self-directed individuals with a strong work ethic'	• Can make informed choices about self-directed play activities and engage in these for a growing amount of time • Can develop open-ended play opportunities	• Can work through a problem with support, beginning to display confidence to facilitate the exploration of learning in the short term • Can understand that learning is taking place	• Can develop own learning experiences • Enjoys success in a variety of ways • Articulates successes in order to take learning further over an extended period
Quality 'Individuals with a well-developed internal model of quality'	• Can say what they like about their own piece of work with encouragement	• Can understand what quality is, and strives to do their best • Can feed back a personal response to others • Is aware that quality exists, and compares own work to that of immediate peer group	• Understands the need to try their best, and experiences a feeling of pride • Can feed back to peers in relation to quality, with suggestions for improvement • Can apply quality criteria to a range of products

Disposition	1	2	3
Character 'Trustworthy individuals with integrity and of ethical character'	• Can make simple choices about right and wrong • Can identify their own needs and those of others, with support • Can respond to 'How would you feel if …?' questions	• Can understand what is right, and behaves accordingly • Can consider the consequences of actions when prompted, in relation to their own needs and those of others	• Understands what is right, and can act and interact honestly • Considers others when making decisions • Can work reliably and is sensitive to others
Collaboration 'Individuals who seek to optimize work through collaboration'	• Can work alongside a group on unthreatening tasks, such as ring games • Enjoys the contributions of others	• Can work as part of a group if offered support • May experience pride on an individual level • Can identify the contributions of other children	• Can work as part of a group, and understands that this is beneficial for all involved • Can build on ideas and experience a feeling of pride for the group • Can understand the benefits of task roles
Curiosity and wonder 'Individuals with a sense of curiosity and wonder'	• Can explore areas of familiar learning • Shows surprise at new concepts which are demonstrated	• Can display curiosity through gestures or facial expressions • With encouragement, can formulate a question to take learning further • Will respond to open questions about their own discoveries	• Can display confidence to question the world • Understands that questioning will lead to learning something new • Can be observant and willing to take risks • Displays joy at new discoveries, often by highlighting these to others
Community 'Responsible and active members of communities'	• Can identify aspects of the FVC (e.g. by looking at the photographs) • Is beginning to understand why the community should work and play safe, hard and fair	• Can contribute to the formulation of the FVC, and knows where this is displayed • Shows concern for a small group of friends • Can carry out specific jobs during tidy-up time	• Can take ownership of class FVC • Shows concern for other members of the group • Contributes to the maintenance of a tidy and orderly setting

There are various different ways of using these indicators in your observation and assessment. A chart or record sheet using these indicators could be arranged in several different ways, as shown opposite. Full sets of each type of record sheet covering all the skills and dispositions are available on the CD-ROM.

1 You could have a sheet for each skill or disposition, with the three level descriptors across the top and a class list down the side. Observations for individual children can be noted, and you can see at a glance those children whom you still need to observe. This type of chart would also give you an 'overall picture' for the whole group.

Class: _____

Details of observation: _____ Date: _____

Problem solving 'Capable of developing effective solutions to the multi-dimensional and complex problems ever present in personal and professional arenas'	• Can acknowledge a problem and think of a solution with adult intervention	• Can independently suggest solutions and can resolve the issue with some support	• Can find an effective solution, communicate this and resolve the issue independently
(Names of children)			

Observation sheet 1

2 Alternatively, a general observation sheet enables you to observe both groups and individuals in relation to the particular skill or disposition.

Observation sheet 2

Observation and assessment of critical skills and fundamental dispositions

Class: _____

Details of observation: _____ Date: _____

Skill or disposition	1	2	3
Group observations		Individual observations	

Critical Skills in the Early Years © Vicki Charlesworth (Network Educational Press, 2005)

Observation
sheet 3

3 Sometimes some prompting is helpful to guide your observations. A format like this, based on the one used in *Education By Design – Tools for the EBD Classroom* (Mobilia, 1998), may be beneficial.

Observation and assessment of critical skills and fundamental dispositions

Class: _____

Date: _____

Details of observation: _____

Skill or disposition	1	2	3

Who talked?

Who listened?

Who followed?

Who led?

Critical Skills in the Early Years   © Vicki Charlesworth (Network Educational Press, 2005)

Bibliography

Black, P. and Wiliam, D. (1998), *Inside the Black Box*, King's College, London School of Education

Black, P. et.al. (2002) *Working Inside the Black Box*, King's College, London School of Education

Call, Nicola (2003) *The Thinking Child*, Network Educational Press

Call, Nicola (2003) *The Thinking Child Resource Book*, Network Educational Press

Cartwright, P., Scott, K. and Stevens, J. (2001) *A Place to Learn – Developing a Stimulating Learning Environment*, Lewisham Early Years Advice and Resource Network

Charlesworth, Vicki (2004) *Helping Young Children to Ask Questions*, Lawrence Educational

Clarke, Shirley (2001) *Unlocking Formative Assessment*, Hodder and Stoughton

DfEE/QCA (2000) *Curriculum Guidance for the Foundation Stage*, ref:QCA/00/587

Institute of Education, *Effective Provision of Pre-School Education*. Findings published at: www.dfes.gov.uk

Evans, B (2002) *You Can't Come To My Party! Conflict Resolution With Young Children*, High/Scope Press

Haynes, Joanna and Murris, Karen (2003) *Storywise: Thinking Through Stories*, Dialogueworks

Mobilia, W. (1998) *Education By Design – Tools for the EBD Classroom*, Network Educational Press

Mobilia, W. (1999) *Education By Design – Level 2 Coaching Kit*, Network Educational Press

Mobilia, W. et al. (1999) *Education By Design – Level 1 Coaching Kit*, Network Educational Press

National Commission for Excellence in Education (1983) *A Nation At Risk*, US Department of Education. A download of this publication is available at: www.ed.go/pubs/NatAtRisk/index.html

Siraj-Blatchford, I. and Sylva, K. (2002) *Researching Effective Pedagogy in the Early Years*, DfES

Useful resources

For details of Kofi the chimpanzee: Bayley, R. and Broadbent, L. (2003) *Helping Young Children to Speak With Confidence*, Lawrence Educational

A useful book for the community building stages: Bedford, D. (2000) *It's My Turn*, Little Tiger Press

Cherrytree Books (1997) Good Manners and Growing Up series, A S Publishing. Titles include *Sharing*, *Taking Turns* and *Being Helpful*

Richardson, J. (1999) *Bad Mood Bear*, Red Fox

Television Junction (2002) *Flip the Bear*. The *Flip the Bear* video and resource pack is available by phoning 0121 248 4466

For more details about the Critical Skills Programme, including training and contacts, see: www.criticalskills.co.uk

CD-ROM resources

Index

A selection of titles from Network Educational Press

ACCELERATED LEARNING SERIES
Accelerated Learning: A User's Guide by Alistair Smith, Mark Lovatt and Derek Wise
Accelerated Learning in Practice by Alistair Smith
The ALPS Approach: accelerated learning in primary schools by Alistair Smith and Nicola Call
The ALPS Approach Resource Book by Alistair Smith and Nicola Call
Reaching out to all learners by Cheshire LEA
Move It by Alistair Smith
Coaching Solutions by Will Thomas and Alistair Smith
Coaching Solutions Resource Book by Will Thomas

EFFECTIVE LEARNING AND LEADERSHIP
Lessons are for Learning by Mike Hughes
Getting Started by Henry Leibling
Closing the Learning Gap by Mike Hughes
Strategies for Closing the Learning Gap by Mike Hughes and Andy Vass
Tweak to Transform by Mike Hughes
Transforming Teaching and Learning by Colin Weatherley, Bruce Bonney, John Kerr and Jo Morrison
Effective Leadership in Schools by Tony Swainston
Leading Change in Schools: A Practical Handbook by Sian Case

ABLE AND TALENTED CHILDREN COLLECTION
Effective Provision for Able and Talented Children by Barry Teare
Effective Resources for Able and Talented Children by Barry Teare
More Effective Resources for Able and Talented Children by Barry Teare
Challenging Resources for Able and Talented Children by Barry Teare
Enrichment Activities for Able and Talented Children by Barry Teare

OTHER TITLES
Towards Successful Learning by Diana Pardoe
Learning to learn for life: research and practical resources for Foundation and Key Stage 1 by Rebecca Goodbourn, Susie Parsons, Julia Wright, Steve Higgins & Kate Wall
Nurturing Independent Thinkers: Working with an alternative curriculum edited by Mike Bosher and Patrick Hazlewood
Moving to Secondary School: Advice and activities to support transition by Lynda Measor with Mike Fleetham
Personalizing Learning: Transforming education for every child by John West-Burnham and Max Coates
The Practical Guide to Revision Techniques by Simon Percival
Future Directions: Practical ways to develop emotional intelligence and confidence in young people by Diane Carrington and Helen Whitten
Discover Your Hidden Talents by Bill Lucas
Help Your Child To Succeed by Bill Lucas and Alistair Smith
Foundations of Literacy by Sue Palmer and Ros Bayley
Flying Start with Literacy: Activities for parents and children by Ros Bayley and Lynn Broadbent
The Thinking Child by Nicola Call with Sally Featherstone
The Thinking Child Resource Book by Nicola Call with Sally Featherstone
But Why? Developing philosophical thinking in the classroom by Sara Stanley with Steve Bowkett
Promoting Children's Well-Being in the Primary Years edited by Andrew Burrell and Jeni Riley
Becoming Emotionally Intelligent by Catherine Corrie
Tooncards: A multi-purpose resource for developing communication skills by Chris Terrell
This is Science! Learning Science through songs and stories (KS1) by Tim Harding
That's Science!, That's Maths! and *That's English! Learning through songs* (KS2) by Tim Harding
With Drama in Mind: Real learning in imagined worlds by Patrice Baldwin
The Brain's Behind It by Alistair Smith
Think it–Map it! by Oliver Caviglioli and Ian Harris
Reaching out to all thinkers by Oliver Caviglioli and Ian Harris
New Tools for Learning: Accelerated learning meets ICT by John Davitt
Exciting ICT in History by Ben Walsh
Exciting ICT in Maths by Alison Clark-Jeavons
Exciting ICT in English by Tony Archdeacon
Seeing History: Visual learning strategies & resources for Key Stage 3 by Tom Haward

For more information and ordering details, please consult our website www.networkpress.co.uk

Network Educational Press – much more than publishing…

NEP Conferences – Invigorate your teaching

Each term NEP runs a wide range of conferences on cutting edge issues in teaching and learning at venues around the UK. The emphasis is always highly practical. Regular presenters include some of our top-selling authors such as Sue Palmer, Barry Teare and Steve Bowkett. Dates and venues for our current programme of conferences can be found on our website www.networkpress.co.uk.

NEP online Learning Style Analysis – Find out how your students prefer to learn

Discovering what makes your students tick is the key to personalizing learning. NEP's Learning Style Analysis is a 50-question online evaluation that can give an immediate and thorough learning profile for every student in your class. It reveals how, when and where they learn best, whether they are right brain or left brain dominant, analytic or holistic, whether they are strongly auditory, visual, kinesthetic or tactile … and a great deal more. And for teachers who'd like to take the next step, LSA enables you to create a whole-class profile for precision lesson planning.

Developed by The Creative Learning Company in New Zealand and based on the work of Learning Styles expert Barbara Prashnig, this powerful tool allows you to analyse your own and your students' learning preferences in a more detailed way than any other product we have ever seen. To find out more about Learning Style Analysis or to order profiles visit www.networkpress.co.uk/lsa.

Also available: *Teaching Style Analysis and Working Style Analysis*

NEP's Critical Skills Programme – Teach your students skills for lifelong learning

The Critical Skills Programme puts pupils at the heart of learning, by providing the skills required to be successful in school and life. Classrooms are developed into effective learning environments, where pupils work collaboratively and feel safe enough to take 'learning risks'. Pupils have more ownership of their learning across the whole curriculum and are encouraged to develop not only subject knowledge but the fundamental skills of:

- problem solving
- creative thinking
- decision making
- communication
- management
- organization
- leadership
- self-direction
- quality working
- collaboration
- enterprise
- community involvement

"The Critical Skills Programme… energizes students to think in an enterprising way. CSP gets students to think for themselves, solve problems in teams, think outside the box, to work in a structured manner. CSP is the ideal way to forge an enterprising student culture."

Rick Lee, Deputy Director, Barrow Community Learning Partnership.

To find out more about CSP training visit the Critical Skills Programme website at www.criticalskills.co.uk